Democracies against Terror

THE WASHINGTON PAPERS

. . . intended to meet the need for an authoritative, yet prompt, public appraisal of the major developments in world affairs.

President, CSIS: David M. Abshire

Series Editor: Walter Laqueur

Director of Publications: Nancy B. Eddy

Managing Editor: Donna R. Spitler

MANUSCRIPT SUBMISSION

The Washington Papers and Praeger Publishers welcome inquiries concerning manuscript submissions. Please include with your inquiry a curriculum vitae, synopsis, table of contents, and estimated manuscript length. Manuscripts must be between 120–200 double-spaced typed pages. All submissions will be peer reviewed. Submissions to *The Washington Papers* should be sent to *The Washington Papers*; The Center for Strategic and International Studies; 1800 K Street NW; Suite 400; Washington, DC 20006. Book proposals should be sent to Praeger Publishers; One Madison Avenue; New York NY 10010.

The Washington Papers/134

Democracies against Terror

The Western Response to State-Supported Terrorism

Geoffrey M. Levitt

Foreword by Walter Laqueur

Published with The Center for
Strategic and International Studies
Washington, D.C.

PRAEGER

New York
Westport, Connecticut
London

Library of Congress Cataloging-in-Publication Data

Levitt, Geoffrey M.
  Democracies against terror : the Western response to state-
supported terrorism / Geoffrey M. Levitt.
     p.   cm. — (The Washington papers, ISSN 0278-937X, vol. XVI, 134)
  "Published with the Center for Strategic and International
Studies, Washington, D.C."
  Bibliography: p.
  Includes index.
  ISBN 0-275-93021-1 (alk. paper). ISBN 0-275-93022-X (pbk. : alk.
paper)
  1. Terrorism — Government policy.   2. Terrorism — Prevention.
3. Security, International.   4. Terrorism — Case studies.   I. Title.
II. Series.
HV6431.L49 1988
363.3'2 — dc19   88-9859

The *Washington Papers* are written under the auspices of The Center
for Strategic and International Studies (CSIS) and published
with CSIS by Praeger Publishers. The views expressed in these papers
are those of the authors and not necessarily those of the Center.

Library of Congress Catalog Card Number: 88-9859
ISBN: 0-275-93021-1 (cloth)
       0-275-93022-X (paper)

First published in 1988

Praeger Publishers, One Madison Avenue, New York, NY 10010
A division of Greenwood Press, Inc.

Printed in the United States of America

The paper used in this book complies with the Permanent
Paper Standard issued by the National Information Standards
Organization (Z39.48-1984).

10   9   8   7   6   5   4   3   2   1

Contents

Foreword

Although state-supported terrorism of one type or another has existed for centuries, it did not become a matter of concern to the international community until the 1970s. The importance of terrorism has occasionally been overrated; it is basically the weapon of the weak and can be applied only infrequently and under specific circumstances. If perpetrated too blatantly, terrorist activity may lead to regular warfare, which is precisely what terrorism's sponsors want to avoid.

There are always exceptions, however. If a country happens to be in a state of anarchy, as has been the case in Lebanon for years, those engaging in state terrorism through surrogates may conclude that the risks they face are greatly diminished. Under such conditions it becomes difficult to attribute responsibility, which in turn makes retaliation impossible. Another potential danger is the use of weapons of mass destruction; such use has not yet occurred, and is unlikely to occur, simply because massive destruction then seems almost inevitable. Unfortunately, however, one cannot completely rely on extremist governments to behave rationally; therefore such a possibility cannot be entirely ruled out.

Because state-supported terrorism has been directed

more often than not against Western governments, it is regrettable that there has not been more cooperation among them. There has been some collaboration, as described in Geoffrey Levitt's pioneering study, mainly in the exchange of information. Such collaboration has led to the arrest of some terrorists and to the prevention of a number of terrorist operations that were planned. Greater cooperation would have had even more impressive results, but this is likely to happen only if terrorist activities should increase.

Such an appraisal of the chances of international cooperation may appear unduly pessimistic. But much experience over the years has shown that with all the existing international agreements, there is always the temptation to strike separate deals with states sponsoring terrorism as long as the incidents are not too frequent. It usually seems the easier way out of a complicated situation fraught with dangers. When the state of affairs deteriorates, there is then much greater willingness to cooperate than in relatively peaceful times.

Geoffrey Levitt is particularly well qualified to provide a balance sheet on state-supported terrorism. He has studied this phenomenon in both theory and practice through his work in the Office of the Legal Adviser of the State Department. He has also had the opportunity to discuss the problems with European officials in the field. Using a number of case studies, he sheds light on both the potential use and present limits of international cooperation. His study is a valuable addition to research in international relations.

Walter Laqueur
Chairman, International Research Council
Center for Strategic and International Studies

March 1988

About the Author

Geoffrey Levitt received his B.A. in political science from Columbia University and holds an M.A. in international affairs (Soviet Union program) from Harvard University and a J.D. from Harvard Law School. He has been a recipient of a John Jay Scholarship from Columbia, a Caroline Cady Hewey Scholarship in International Affairs from Harvard, and a Hubert H. Humphrey Fellowship from the U.S. Arms Control and Disarmament Agency. He also holds a certificate in Russian language and literature from the Pushkin Language Institute in Moscow.

Since 1981 he has worked at the Office of the Legal Adviser, U.S. Department of State, where he has served as counsel to the Bureau of European and Canadian Affairs (1981–1983) and to the Office for Combatting Terrorism (1983–1986). He was selected as an international affairs fellow in 1986–1987 by the Council on Foreign Relations and during that year worked concurrently as a visiting scholar at CSIS. He has published several articles on the legal aspects of terrorism and of U.S.-Soviet relations.

Acknowledgments

This project would not have been possible without the support of the Council on Foreign Relations. Its International Affairs Fellowship program provided a unique opportunity for a harried bureaucrat to spend a year thinking, researching, and writing. The two individuals in charge of this worthwhile program, Kempton Dunn and Alton Frye, deserve special recognition. At the Center for Strategic and International Studies, Walter Laqueur was very generous of his precious time and formidable intellectual resources; Dr. Robert Kupperman also kindly shared his own profound knowledge of the topic and made available indispensable administrative support. Among colleagues from the State Department, Ambassador Robert Oakley provided key inspiration for the project, and Ambassador Parker Borg's efforts to clarify, sharpen, and generally improve the manuscript were tremendously helpful. Professor John Murphy of Villanova University Law School also contributed substantively to the final product. A special word of gratitude is further owed to those government officials experienced in counterterrorism in the United States and Europe who graciously consented to speak with me as part of the research for the project. And finally, the most heartfelt thanks go to my wife, Dr. Karen Collias, whose finely honed professional research skills and unflagging support were all-important to the completion of this study. The responsibility for its content, of course, is mine alone.

G.M.L.

Summary

This book examines one of the West's most ambitious, effective, and potentially powerful attempts to combat international terrorism — cooperation among the non-Communist world's seven largest economic and political powers. This group, known as the Summit Seven, has met at the summit level every year since 1975, rotating between the capitals of its member states. It possesses no formal structure, no permanent staff, and no charter, and it focuses primarily on economic rather than political issues. Yet the group has so far issued seven joint declarations on terrorism; it has also made serious efforts to impose coordinated multilateral sanctions against states that have supported terrorism. Today the Summit Seven framework is still a major avenue of U.S. policy on international cooperation against terrorism, despite the disappointments and frustrations that have plagued the group's counterterrorism efforts.

The study traces Summit Seven initiatives on terrorism since the group began to focus on the issue in 1978. It examines the summit declarations on various forms of terrorism and describes the political and technical follow-up to these declarations by the governments involved. It then analyzes the responses of the Seven governments, jointly and individually, to six selected terrorist incidents. Finally, conclusions are drawn about the essential elements of a collective response to state-supported terrorism.

Democracies against Terror

Introduction

The dangers of state-supported terrorism are by now all too familiar.[1] A state that makes its resources – financial, logistical, training, intelligence, and political – available for terrorism vastly enhances the striking power of terrorists. Of even more profound concern is the damage done by state-supported terrorism to the fragile international order. State support is what helps to transform terrorism from an intelligence and law enforcement problem into an international political threat.

This book examines efforts by the major Western democracies to cooperate in isolating, deterring, and punishing states that support international terrorism. The primary, though not exclusive, focus will be on U.S. policy during the Reagan administration.

Following this introduction, which assesses the importance of international cooperation in overall U.S. terrorism policy, the first chapter looks at terrorism itself from an international perspective. What exactly is it that the Western democracies claim to be fighting? Despite a good deal of international disagreement about terrorism, there is nonetheless a significant degree of formal international consensus on the subject. Such consensus, moreover, is an essential element in international cooperation to combat terrorism.

The next two chapters describe the efforts of the Western democracies to apply or enforce some of the international norms described in the first chapter: The second chapter discusses the main joint declarations of the United States and its major democratic allies in relation to specific categories of terrorism; the third examines the collective actions of these states in response to selected terrorist incidents that fall within those categories. Finally, the fourth chapter will draw some conclusions about the essential elements of a collective response to state-supported terrorism.

Few of the many truisms about terrorism are repeated more often or more fervently than the need for international cooperation to combat it. International cooperation has been a central ideal of U.S. counterterrorism policy since its beginning; as the focus on terrorism has intensified during the 1980s, U.S. government officials at all levels have consistently stressed this ideal.

Soon after the Reagan administration assumed office, Secretary of State Alexander M. Haig, Jr. declared:

> International terrorism will take the place of human rights, our concern, because it is the ultimate abuse of human rights. And it's time that it be addressed with greater clarity and greater effectiveness by Western nations and the United States as well.[2]

This declaration signaled the Reagan administration's intensified focus on terrorism in general and international counterterrorism cooperation in particular. A statement later in 1981 before the Senate Foreign Relations Committee amplified the executive branch's thinking:

> As to international cooperation, it is clear that combatting international terrorism is not a task for the United States alone. The problem is too complex and universal to be dealt with by any one nation. We are committed to working with other nations to establish a peaceful

and stable world order, in which we may be free from
the threat of political violence.... [T]his administration has given a high priority to this task.[3]

President Reagan himself has on several occasions emphasized the importance of international counterterrorism
cooperation. In his 1984 State of the Union address, for
example, the president said: "We must not be driven from
our objectives ... by state-sponsored terrorism." "This ugly
specter," he went on, "demands international attention ... I
will be seeking support from our allies for concerted action."[4] More recently this theme of international cooperation
has continued to resonate in U.S. pronouncements about
counterterrorism. As Secretary of State George P. Shultz
put it in a February 1985 speech: "The enemies of the West
are united. So, too, must the democratic countries be united
in a common defense against terrorism."[5] Ambassador-at-
Large for Counter-Terrorism L. Paul Bremer III summa-
rized the theme at a conference in January 1987:

> We must work with friendly states to make it clear that
> we will not conduct business as usual with states sup-
> porting terrorism. Simply put, the community of na-
> tions must increase the political, economic, and, yes,
> perhaps even the military, costs of helping terrorists
> until the sponsoring states can no longer afford to pay
> them.[6]

Congress, too, has focused on the need for international
cooperation in counterterrorism. The Omnibus Diplomatic
Security and Antiterrorism Act of 1986, for instance, contained an entire title on "Multilateral Cooperation to Combat International Terrorism," a section of which directed the
president to seek the formation of an "International Anti-
Terrorism Committee" consisting of representatives of the
North Atlantic Treaty Organization (NATO) countries, Japan, "and such other countries as may be invited and may
choose to participate." This directive was based on findings
that

(1) international terrorism is and remains a serious threat to the peace and security of free, democratic nations;

(2) the challenge of terrorism can only be met effectively by concerted action on the part of all responsible nations. . . . [7]

Even this cursory survey reveals a strong theme in the attitude of the U.S. government toward international counterterrorism: for cooperation, the United States looks first and foremost to its major Western allies. And a moment's reflection reveals that there are solid, unsentimental reasons for such an orientation. First, the United States and its allies have been among the chief targets of state-supported terrorism — which is not only a grave violation of international norms, but also a form of political violence against the Western democracies by certain governments with fundamentally hostile interests and philosophies. The corollary is that the democracies have a special stake in banding together to combat state-supported terrorism — not only because it threatens their immediate political interests or the safety of their citizens, but because on a deeper level it represents a serious challenge to their avowed common orientation toward a more stable and peaceful international order.

Second, given their political and economic weight on the world scene, the Western democracies are uniquely able to apply the collective pressures that can demonstrate meaningful opposition to state-supported terrorism. As an official commented during the 1987 Venice meeting of the countries of the Summit Seven, "Tensions here, tensions there . . . where are people supposed to look for solutions if not to the assembled political firepower of the free world?"[8] Lone political action against state-supported terrorism, even by the United States, has inherent limitations. But if the democracies support each other, they send a strong signal of unity and resolve to the direct object of their attention as well as to other governments that might consider acting irresponsibly. Conversely, disunity among those states that are the major target of international terrorism can only embolden the state supporters of that terrorism — and for that matter, other hostile states — encouraging them to treat the West with contempt and to play upon divisions among the democracies.

Finally, the visibility and emotional impact of terrorism inevitably make it an acid test for relations among the major Western powers in general. Few other issues can lead to such intense friction among friendly governments. The feelings of betrayal and frustration that can result from being "let down" by an ally in responding to a state-supported terrorist threat can run rather deep, matched on the other side by the fear of being "dragged into" overly aggressive actions with unpredictable and dangerous results. It is doubtful that the Western partnership would come to an end over a failure to coordinate counterterrorism policies, but the cumulative effect of such failures on the mutual trust and respect necessary for good relations among the major democracies should not be underestimated. This problem makes international cooperation against terrorism an issue of concern going beyond counterterrorism policy itself.

1

What Is Terrorism?

To combat state-supported terrorism effectively requires a clear idea of what is being opposed – not to set legalistic guidelines for defining specific terrorist incidents, but to provide a conceptual basis for the necessary collective response to this threat. Such a response, if it is to be anything more than an ad hoc exercise of power based on short-term national self-interest, must relate to some external, established standards violated by the terrorist state.

Two basic approaches have been used to define such standards at the international level. The deductive approach sets forth a single, analytical definition to cover all acts the definer wishes to consider as terrorist. A typical example is the following proposal: "Terrorism is the deliberate and systematic murder, maiming, and menacing of the innocent to inspire fear for political ends."[1] Such definitions – and many have been advanced – may serve inspirational and political ends, but as a direct basis for practical collective responses to international terrorism they are inherently so broad, vague, and controversial as to be practically useless.

The second method – the inductive approach – has thus yielded the only real progress. It delineates a series of specific categories of criminal acts that together compose an

open-ended framework to define terrorism, without necessarily even using the term explicitly. States that may not be
able to agree on an overall definition of terrorism can agree
that a specific category of criminal acts constitutes unacceptable behavior. By this method, several of the most prevalent forms of international terrorism – aircraft hijacking,
aircraft sabotage, attacks on diplomats, and hostage-taking – have been defined through treaties as criminal offenses of international significance.[2] These treaties, though
imperfect and partial, nonetheless provide a real basis for
international enforcement efforts against terrorism.

Another set of existing international obligations –
those covering diplomatic privileges and immunities – also
directly applies to this subject, because certain states have
systematically abused such privileges and immunities as a
means of aiding terrorist activities. These obligations also
form part of the framework of international norms relevant
to state-supported terrorism.

The foregoing does not imply that governments confronted with state-supported terrorism should wait for the
United Nations (UN) General Assembly to furnish the precise legal definition of the problem before they can take
collective measures against it. Nor does it say that when
governments act against state-supported terrorism, even in
an area where there is a specific international instrument
such as aircraft hijacking, their actions necessarily are or
should be within the precise ambit of the relevant instrument. But it does affirm the development of a framework of
international norms that governments ostensibly seek to
uphold when they act against state-supported terrorism.
Narrow national self-interest, domestic politics, and so
forth of course play a role in counterterrorism as in all areas
of policy. But these established standards provide a necessary external frame of reference within which various governments can coalesce to take effective collective action
against state supporters of terrorism.

The remainder of this chapter describes these standards and the process of their creation in more detail. The

specific categories covered represent a basic checklist of some of the most important existing formal standards relating to international terrorism. By enumerating the types of acts that have explicitly been labeled illegitimate at the international level, these categories form a basic framework for supplying specific content to the concept of international terrorism.

Aviation Terrorism

When terrorist attacks on civil aviation erupted in the fall of 1970, the international community reacted swiftly by concluding the Convention for the Suppression of Unlawful Seizure of Aircraft at The Hague on December 16, 1970. The Hague Convention defined the offense of unlawful seizure of aircraft, obligated parties to establish criminal jurisdiction over the offense when committed under specified jurisdictional circumstances, and established the extradite-or-prosecute requirement that was to become the foundation of all similar future international legal efforts pertaining to various categories of "terrorist" offenses.[3]

This achievement, of course, was not written on a blank slate. The preceding year had witnessed a series of steps in the UN and in the International Civil Aviation Organization (ICAO), a specialized UN agency, that indicated a drastically heightened international sensitivity to the issue of unlawful interference with civil aviation. In December 1969 the General Assembly had adopted, by 77 to 2 with 17 abstentions, a resolution on "Forcible Diversion of Civil Aircraft in Flight," which called upon states "to take every appropriate measure to ensure that their respective national legislations provide an adequate framework for effective legal measures against all kinds of acts of unlawful interference with, seizure of, or other wrongful exercise of control by force or threat thereof over civil aircraft in flight." It urged states "in particular to ensure that persons on board who perpetrate such acts are prosecuted" and urged "full support" for ICAO efforts toward "the speedy preparation and implementation" of the instrument that would become the Hague Convention.[4] In the summer of 1970, the ICAO convened an Extraordinary Assembly that adopted 24 resolutions on various aspects of aviation security and unlawful interference with aircraft.[5] One of these resolutions noted the "urgent need for an international convention as a means of dealing more effectively with the unlawful seizure of aircraft" and called upon states attending the ICAO diplomatic conference scheduled for December of that year "to make every reasonable effort . . . to agree on a convention based on the draft convention" prepared and approved earlier in the year by the ICAO Legal Committee.[6] On the eve of the ICAO conference, the UN General Assembly adopted, by 105 to 0 with 8 abstentions, a resolution on "aerial hijacking or interference with civil air travel" condemning "without exception whatsoever, all acts of aerial hijacking or other interference with civil air travel . . . through the use or threat of force," and strongly supporting the ongoing ICAO efforts to create legal mechanisms to suppress skyjacking.[7]

One aspect of ICAO's work in the period leading up to the conclusion of the Hague Convention is particularly relevant to this discussion. A resolution adopted by the ICAO Council on October 1, 1970 called upon member states

> to ensure the safety and security of international civil air transport, upon request of a Contracting State to consult together immediately with a view to deciding what joint action should be undertaken, in accordance with international law, *without excluding measures such as the suspension of international civil air transport services to and from any State* which after the unlawful seizure of an aircraft, detains passengers, crew or aircraft . . . for international blackmail purposes, or any State which . . . fails to extradite or prosecute persons committing acts of unlawful seizure for international blackmail purposes.[8]

The resolution directed the ICAO Legal Committee to consider "an international convention or other international instruments" to "give effect to the purposes" of the paragraph above. The Legal Committee's work on this resolution would ultimately fall short of the ambition reflected in it. But the concept of an international civil aviation boycott against a state that failed to honor its international obligations for handling the aftermath of a skyjacking incident — the concept on which, eight years later, the Bonn Antihijacking Declaration of the Summit Seven would be based — had been officially expressed.

Within the ICAO framework itself, however, expressing the idea of an aviation boycott would prove easier than putting such a boycott into practice. The Legal Committee's work in response to the October 1970 Council resolution initially centered around a U.S. draft proposal for a convention to provide for mandatory joint action against a state determined by a fact-finding commission to have failed to extradite a hijacker found within its territory or to submit the case to its competent authorities for the purpose of prosecution. Such joint action could include suspension of all international aviation to and from the defaulting state.[9] But in its work over the next three years on the U.S. draft, as well as on other proposals to establish international machinery to promote enforcement of obligations concerning skyjacking, the ICAO Legal Committee was unable to agree on any new measures.[10] The ICAO conference held in Rome in 1973 to consider several of these proposals also ended in failure, plagued by the same philosophical divisions that had undermined other UN efforts to grapple with the issue of terrorism.[11] Thus the Hague Convention was left with only the weakest of internal enforcement devices — its own more or less standard dispute settlement clause, providing that disputes over the interpretation or application of the convention that could not be settled through negotiation would be submitted to arbitration and then if necessary to the International Court of Justice (Article 11). There is no record of this clause ever having been invoked.

The early 1970s nevertheless did see one other notable success in ICAO's work against unlawful interference with civil aviation. This was the Convention for the Suppression of Unlawful Acts against the Safety of Civil Aviation, concluded at Montreal on September 23, 1971. Its extradite-or-prosecute structure was like that of the Hague Convention; instead of unlawful seizure of aircraft, however, the Montreal Convention dealt with various unlawful acts that would endanger the safety of an aircraft in flight.[12] Like the Hague Convention, the Montreal Convention was framed in response to an escalation of the relevant type of terrorist violence, in particular the bombings of Austrian and Swiss airliners the previous year.[13]

Attacks on Internationally Protected Persons

Attacking diplomats — often by hostage-taking, but by assassination and other forms of assault as well — has been a favored method of international terrorists. From the terrorist's point of view, such attacks yield a double satisfaction: they symbolically strike at the victim's government in a way that is instantly recognizable, and they embarrass the government of the country in which the attack takes place (assuming that government is not itself behind the attack). Although this type of terrorism has waned somewhat in recent years, its use is still significant; during the late 1970s and early 1980s it was actually the most prominent form of international terrorism.

The first organized international effort in the postwar period to address the problem of terrorist attacks on diplomats was undertaken in the Organization of American States (OAS). Prompted by an ominous increase in the frequency and severity of terrorist acts in the Americas, the OAS on February 2, 1971 concluded the "Convention to Prevent and Punish the Acts of Terrorism Taking the Form of Crimes against Persons and Related Extortion That Are of International Significance."[14] This convention defined a class of "common crimes of international significance," consisting of "kidnapping, murder, and other assaults against the life or personal integrity of those persons to whom the state has the duty to give special protection according to international law, as well as extortion in connection with those crimes" (Article 2).[15] Persons charged with or convicted of such crimes would be subject to extradition, or when an extradition request in such a case was "not in order because the person sought is a national of the requested state, or because of some other legal or constitutional impediment," the state where the alleged offender was located would be obliged to submit the case to its own authorities for prosecution, "as if the act had been committed in its own territory" (Articles 3 and 5). The contracting states also undertook various cooperative measures to prevent and punish the offenses covered by the convention (Article 8).

The OAS Convention on Terrorism, hampered by vague definitions and gaping loopholes, did not prove a very efficacious document.[16] Its historical importance, however, lies less in its own results than in its role as a model and spur for a more significant international effort along the same lines. As an outgrowth of the enhanced attention to international terrorism during the Twenty-Seventh UN General Assembly in 1972, during the following General Assembly session the Sixth Committee (Legal) set to work on the text of a convention to address the threat of terrorism against internationally protected persons, including diplomats. Among the sources drawn upon in the development of this convention were draft articles prepared by the International Law Commission, the Hague and Montreal Conventions on aviation terrorism, the Vienna Convention on Diplomatic Relations (which defined the category of diplomatic agents and codified the special duty of states to provide for their protection), and the OAS Convention.[17]

The political divisions that had consistently undermined the General Assembly's handling of the terrorism issue also haunted UN work on the Internationally Protected Persons Convention. On the eve of full General Assembly consideration of the draft convention late in 1973, certain delegations proposed a new article making the convention "inapplicable" to acts committed by "peoples struggling against colonialism, alien domination, foreign occupation, racial discrimination and apartheid in the exercise of their legitimate rights to self-determination and independence."[18] Adoption of the convention nearly foundered on this proposal. But through a series of ingenious maneuvers it was transformed, in watered-down form, into part of the (nonbinding) resolution under which the convention was to be adopted, rather than becoming part of the convention itself; failure was thus averted, and on December 14, 1973 the General Assembly approved and adopted the text of the Convention on the Prevention and Punishment of Crimes against Internationally Protected Persons, Including Diplomatic Agents.[19]

The convention defines the class of internationally protected persons as including heads of state, heads of government, and foreign ministers, as well as accompanying family members, whenever such persons are in a foreign state, and any representative or official of a state or an international organization who, "at the time when and in the place where a crime against him . . . is committed, is entitled pursuant to international law to special protection from any attack on his person, freedom or dignity," as well as "members of his family forming part of his household" (Article 1[1]). The latter class primarily comprises diplomats and consuls entitled to special protection according to the applicable international conventions.[20] All states must establish legal jurisdiction under specified circumstances over the intentional commission of certain violent crimes against an internationally protected person, including murder, kidnapping, or other attack upon the person or liberty of such an individual. As with the other antiterrorism conventions, the heart of the Internationally Protected Persons Convention is its requirement that a state either extradite an alleged offender or submit his case for prosecution (Article 7).

Beyond these purely penal provisions, states party to the convention are also required to cooperate in preventing the relevant crimes (Article 4). Finally, this convention contains the usual dispute settlement clause (Article 13), for practical purposes identical to those of the other conventions described above. As with the other terrorism conventions, there is no record of this clause having been used.

The Internationally Protected Persons Convention has been fairly widely subscribed to, though not as universally as the air terrorism conventions: as of this writing there were nearly 70 parties representing all major segments of the international community.[21]

Hostage-Taking

As the wave of hostage-taking reached its crest in the mid-1970s, the UN began to consider measures to counter this threat. At the thirty-first session of the General Assembly in 1976, West Germany proposed that an international convention against the taking of hostages be drafted.[22] The task was assigned to an ad hoc committee, which, after fiercely debating such issues as the treatment of national liberation movements and the right to use force to end a hostage-taking incident, put forward a draft convention that was adopted by the General Assembly on December 19, 1979 as the International Convention against the Taking of Hostages.[23]

This convention defines the offense of hostage-taking as the seizing or detaining and threatening to kill, injure, or continue to detain another person (the hostage) to compel a third party to do or abstain from doing any act as a condition for the release of the hostage (Article 1). Parties to the convention must make the offense punishable by "appropriate penalties" that take into account its "grave nature" (Article 2). A state party in whose territory a hostage is held "shall take all measures it considers appropriate to ease the situation of the hostage, in particular, to secure his release"

(Article 3); state parties are also to cooperate in preventing hostage-taking from occurring in the first place (Article 4). The essence of the convention, as with the other global antiterrorism conventions, is the obligation to establish criminal jurisdiction over the offense under a wide range of circumstances and either to extradite or prosecute the alleged offender (Article 8).

Certain issues that were politically contentious during the drafting of the convention were handled in its text in a manner that distinguishes it from the earlier antiterrorism conventions. First, Article 12 provides that the convention does not apply to acts of hostage-taking "committed in the course of armed conflicts as defined in the Geneva Conventions of 1949 and the protocols thereto, including armed conflicts . . . in which peoples are fighting against colonial domination and alien occupation and against racist regimes in the exercise of their right of self-determination." This exclusion only applies, however, if states party to the Hostages Convention are bound by the former conventions to prosecute or hand over the hostage-taker. Thus, despite its aggressive national liberation rhetoric, this provision creates no gap in the legal coverage of the offense.[24] Second, Article 14 addresses the issue that became known during the negotiations as the "anti-Entebbe clause": "Nothing in this Convention shall be construed as justifying the violation of the territorial integrity or political independence of a State in contravention of the Charter of the United Nations."[25] Third, Article 9 prohibits a state from granting an extradition request if that state has "substantial grounds" for believing that the request was made "for the purpose of prosecuting or punishing a person on account of his race, religion, nationality, ethnic origin or political opinion."[26]

Finally, the convention is provided with a more or less standard (and so far unused) procedure (Article 16) submitting unsettled disputes "concerning the interpretation or application of this Convention" to arbitration and on to the International Court of Justice if the parties cannot agree on the organization of the arbitration.[27]

By the fall of 1987, the Hostages Convention had some 40 adherents, with a fairly broad representation of the international community.[28] Because hostage-taking continues to be prevalent, the UN has continued to look at the issue. In December 1985 the Security Council adopted a resolution unequivocally condemning "all acts of hostage-taking and abduction," calling for the "immediate safe release of all hostages . . . wherever and by whomever they are being held," appealing to all states not yet party to the Hostages Convention to "consider the possibility" of adhering to it, and urging international cooperation "to facilitate the prevention, prosecution and punishment of all acts of hostage-taking and abduction as manifestations of international terrorism."[29]

Terrorist Abuse of Diplomatic Immunities

The diplomatic privileges and immunities codified in the Vienna Convention on Diplomatic Relations are expressly intended "not to benefit individuals but to ensure the efficient performance of the functions of diplomatic missions" (Preamble). They have nevertheless been used on occasion as a protective screen for the planning, preparation, and commission of terrorist acts.[30] The Vienna Convention provides several types of immunities that might lend themselves to this sort of abuse: the inviolability of the mission premises, which agents of the host country may not enter except with the consent of the head of the mission (Article 22); the personal inviolability of the diplomatic courier and the prohibition against opening or detaining the diplomatic bag (Article 27); the personal inviolability of the diplomatic agent, who is not liable to any form of arrest or detention (Article 29); and the immunity of the diplomatic agent from the criminal jurisdiction of the country in which he is accredited. (Article 31).[31] Under these protections, weapons or explosives for use in a terrorist act could be brought into a country secretly and stored on mission premises without the interference or even the knowledge of the host country's authorities. A diplomatic agent could act as an accomplice, coconspirator, or actual participant in a criminal terrorist act without any liability to arrest or prosecution.[32]

The Vienna Convention does not, however, leave the host country totally defenseless. Any diplomat may be at any time and without explanation declared persona non grata, at which time his government must either recall the diplomat or terminate his functions with the mission. If it refuses or fails to carry out these obligations within a reasonable time, the host country may refuse to recognize the diplomat as a member of the mission, which would entail a loss of diplomatic protection (Article 9). The declaration of nonacceptability may even be made before the person in question arrives at his post. Therefore, although the host country is barred from using some of its normal law enforcement techniques to combat terrorism committed by foreign diplomats, it does at least have recourse to quick expulsion or exclusion of a diplomat suspected of actual or potential involvement in terrorist activities. Further, it may control the size of a foreign mission in its territory, requiring that size be kept within limits it considers "reasonable and normal" (Article 11). The smaller the mission size, the easier it is to monitor mission members who may have a propensity for involvement in terrorist activities. Both the 1984 London and 1986 Tokyo summit declarations, discussed in chapter 2, emphasized the use of these powers by the host government as a counterterrorism measure.

Finally, all the protections of the Vienna Convention are subject to the following obligations (Article 41):

> 1. Without prejudice to their privileges and immunities, it is the duty of all persons enjoying such privileges and immunities to respect the laws and regulations of the receiving State. They also have a duty not to interfere in the internal affairs of that State. . . .
>
> 3. The premises of the mission must not be used in any manner incompatible with the functions of the mis-

sion as laid down in the present Convention or by other
rules of general international law. . . .

As the words "without prejudice" make clear, these obligations of course cannot be used by the host country to
overturn the structure of privileges and immunities itself.
But serious abuses by diplomats might provide a legal basis for limited retaliation to redress the damage caused by
such abuses. Suppose, for example, that automatic weapon
fire coming from the premises of a mission was endangering
the public. Government authorities, under the provisions
cited above as well as under the inherent right of self-defense, would have the right forcibly to suppress the source
of fire even if such action technically violated the mission
premises — as long as the action taken was consistent with
the basic self-defense doctrines of necessity, proportional-
ity, and discrimination.

Clearly the main factor compelling strict observance of
the privileges and immunities of the Vienna Convention is
reciprocity. When a terrorist act causes an emergency, the
responsible authorities will probably respond as they see fit
and let the Foreign Ministry pick up the legal and political
pieces. In less clear-cut cases, however, a government's willingness to act aggressively toward diplomats suspected of
involvement in terrorism is likely to be conditioned as much
by fears of retaliation against its own diplomats (or, for that
matter, other nationals) as by any other consideration. Of
course, a state can always protect itself from terrorist abuse
of diplomatic privileges and immunities by the simple if
radical expedient of breaking diplomatic relations with the
state that has sent the diplomats. Obviously this may have
political costs, but if the terrorist threat is great enough the
government may decide to bear those costs, as Great Britain did with regard to Syria in October 1986.

Amending the Vienna Convention to make it easier to
deter and punish terrorist abuse of diplomatic privileges
and immunities has been considered in some quarters. A
resolution introduced in the U.S. Congress has proposed, for

example, that "the President of the United States should seek a re-negotiation of the Vienna Convention as to immunity from criminal jurisdiction with the objective of amending article 31 to exempt from such immunity murder and other grave crimes involving assault with firearms or explosives."[33] The British government also examined this question in the wake of the April 1984 Libyan People's Bureau incident in London. But both U.S. and UK officials have been quite cold toward possible renegotiation of the convention, noting the disproportionate dangers for their own diplomats inherent in any loosening of the criminal immunity standard, as well as the tremendous political and procedural difficulties such an effort would encounter in the first place.[34]

Conclusion

Although the foregoing framework of international norms is important, from the perspective of state-supported terrorism, it is incomplete in two important respects. First, this framework does not directly address certain types of very serious terrorist acts, such as bombings or assassinations. Obviously, however, such acts cannot be, and are not, omitted from consideration in counterterrorism policy merely because they have not yet been defined with the same degree of formality and specificity as those outlined above. Second, and most germane to this discussion, the framework provides no effective enforcement mechanisms against states that support terrorism or provide sanctuary to those who commit terrorist acts. The only effort in this direction is the standard dispute settlement clauses contained in the conventions themselves, which may be of some use in civil aviation or trade agreements but are inadequate in an area as politically charged and sensitive as terrorism. The existing framework of legal standards relating to international terrorism is, in fact, centered almost entirely upon the acts of individuals. How can these standards be applied to the activities of states?

Efforts to specify international norms against state involvement in terrorism go back at least as far as 1937. In that year the Convention for the Prevention and Punishment of Terrorism was concluded under the auspices of the League of Nations.[35] Article 1 of the convention (signed by 23 states but never entered into force) explicitly reaffirms "the principle of international law in virtue of which it is the duty of every State to refrain from any act designed to encourage terrorist activities directed against another State."

But it would not be until many years later that the League's successor organization would officially voice this principle, and then not in a treaty but only in the form of a nonbinding declaration. On October 24, 1970 the UN General Assembly adopted the Declaration of Principles of International Law Concerning Friendly Relations and Cooperation among States in Accordance with the Charter of the United Nations.[36] That declaration contained this statement:

> Every State has the duty to refrain from organizing, instigating, assisting or participating in acts of civil strife or terrorist acts in another State or acquiescing in organized activities within its territory directed toward the commission of those acts, when the acts referred to in the present paragraph involve a threat or use of force.

This statement in turn was tied to the fundamental principle stated in the declaration, derived directly from Article 2(4) of the UN Charter, that "States shall refrain in their international relations from the threat or use of force against the territorial integrity or political independence of any State, or in any other manner inconsistent with the purposes of the United Nations." But although the principle that states should refrain from terrorism was easy enough for governments of the UN to agree upon, its specific meaning and application were quite a different matter. Yes, state involvement in terrorism was wrong, but what exactly was it? As UN efforts to define and address international terrorism continued in the 1970s, it quickly became evident that the conceptual and political gulf between different segments of the international community on this issue was vast.[37]

More recently, however, a measure of conceptual progress has been achieved at the UN level. A December 1985 General Assembly resolution on international terrorism for the first time directly linked the duty of states to refrain from involvement in "terrorist acts" to the specific criminal actions – aircraft hijacking and sabotage, attacks on diplomats, and hostage-taking – previously addressed by the international community in a counterterrorism context.[38] This resolution, admittedly a tentative initial step, yielded two positive results: it provided, at the broadest international level, specific, agreed-upon content for the (still quite incomplete) notion of state-supported terrorism; and it demonstrated the continuing trend of international opinion toward building a conceptual framework to delegitimize international terrorism and state involvement in it.

The move from a recognition of the significant and growing – though still far from perfect – international framework of counterterrorism standards to the actual enforcement of such standards is, however, far from automatic. The existence of ostensibly neutral international norms does not in itself mean that the entire international community has an equal, common interest in observing or enforcing these norms. A closer look at the debates that took place during the early period of the international community's attention to the issue of terrorism helps reveal why it is the Western democracies that have been forced to take on the lion's share of the task of upholding the standards against this form of political violence and why certain other states with political interests and philosophies fundamentally opposed to those of the liberal democracies have been among its chief instigators.

As terrorism burst upon the international scene at the beginning of the 1970s, those states that felt most threatened began to look for ways to secure the international cooperation perceived to be necessary to defeat this new menace.[39] Quite naturally, the UN structure was the starting point for this search. It soon became apparent, however, that from the perspective of Western governments the role of the UN in international counterterrorism cooperation would at best be severely limited. In 1972, responding to the upsurge in terrorist incidents and particularly the massacre of Israeli athletes at the Munich Olympics, UN Secretary General Kurt Waldheim undertook a special initiative to bring the issue of international terrorism before the General Assembly.[40] The United States played a very active role in this UN effort; Secretary of State William P. Rogers gave special attention to the problem in his speech before the 27th General Assembly in September:

> In short, the issue is whether the vulnerable lines of international communication . . . can continue, without disruption, to bring nations and peoples together. All who have a stake in this have a stake in decisive action to suppress these demented acts of terrorism.[41]

At the same time the United States circulated a draft "Convention for the Prevention and Punishment of Certain Acts of International Terrorism," which sought to establish an international regime for the legal suppression of the most serious acts of terrorist violence.[42]

But the General Assembly resolution that emerged from that session was unsatisfactory to the United States and many of its allies. Heavily slanted toward justifying the legitimacy of the armed struggle of the "national liberation movements" and condemning the "colonial, racist and alien regimes" against which these movements were fighting, Resolution 3034 was adopted by 76 votes to 35, with 17 abstentions. The United States and most of its allies voted against the resolution.[43] The subsequent work of the ad hoc Committee on International Terrorism established by Resolution 3034 was of little comfort to governments that looked for a strong UN antiterrorism stance. The committee was unable to agree either on the definition of terrorism, its causes, or methods to prevent it; not surprisingly, the U.S. draft convention did not survive the committee process.[44]

In the wake of this abortive attempt to tackle international terrorism on a global level, those states that were more interested in achieving effective counterterrorism measures than in listening to national liberation rhetoric realized that they would have to work through forums other than the UN. The Parliamentary Assembly of the Council of Europe (COE) spoke frankly in October 1972, as the direction of the current at the UN was becoming evident: "It can be concluded, therefore, that although the [terrorism] problem is a universal one, the lack of solidarity at the United Nations level makes it all the more necessary for coordinated action to be taken at the West European level."[45]

As the statement indicates, during this period perceptions of the international terrorism problem began to change. An earlier view prevalent in Western governmental circles had been that terrorism was a common global scourge, with an ideological element to be sure, but nonetheless somehow outside the bounds of politics as usual—a sort of political public health emergency to be combatted in a neutral, technical fashion by the "international community" as a whole, as reflected in Secretary Rogers's characterization of terrorist acts as "demented."

But as the UN discussions on terrorism continued, and as incident after incident made the anti-Western orientation of international terrorism more and more evident, a new perception was emerging in some Western quarters: a view of terrorism as a tactic used by some members of the international community—namely, certain radical Third World and socialist bloc governments – against other members, primarily the Western democracies and their friends around the world. The notion that there were intractable differences of interest and principle between the Western democracies on the one hand and certain radical Third World and socialist states on the other regarding international terrorism (a conclusion difficult to avoid in the face of the experiences of Resolution 3034 and the ad hoc Committee on International Terrorism) was evident in certain pronouncements by Western authorities as early as 1972–1973. As the COE Parliamentary Assembly put it: "The resolution (3034) passed by the UN against terrorism . . . was ineffective because more States favoured terrorism and frustrated joint international action against it. . . . "[46] A U.S. official directly involved in these UN efforts similarly expressed the view that "there were some states who did not wish to take any action at all on this problem. . . . Some few of those states frankly espoused the employment of terroristic methods as a part of their revolutionary philosophy."[47]

The obvious corollary of the new perception of terrorism as an anti-Western campaign was that the democracies would have to work together to defend themselves against this method of attack. And indeed, during the 1970s terrorism came to be placed on the agenda, with varying degrees of urgency, of the major Western political "clubs" – the COE, the European Communities (EC), and NATO.[48] In this light it was almost inevitable that the issue would come to the attention of the most exclusive – and in some ways the most powerful and prestigious – Western grouping of all: the Summit Seven. From the perspective of U.S. counterterrorism policy, this group is particularly important, as the Summit Seven is the only multilateral framework that brings together the United States and its major democratic allies – Canada, West Germany, France, Italy, Japan, and the United Kingdom – with a mandate potentially broad enough to address this issue. The next chapter examines the Summit Seven and its main declarations on international terrorism.

2

The Language of Cooperation: The Summit Seven Declarations

An effective collective response to state-supported terrorism requires not only a common understanding of the threat such terrorism poses, but also an awareness of credible and viable channels for responding to it. For the United States, as the 1986 report of the Vice President's Task Force on Combatting Terrorism put it, "the best multilateral forum for the discussion of terrorism [has been found] to be the industrialized democracies which constitute the Summit Seven."[1] It is not hard to see why this is so. Global structures such as the UN and its affiliated organs, though important for building consensus, for concluding formal antiterrorism instruments, and for pursuing technical security measures in channels such as the ICAO, are simply too big and too politically diverse to adopt effective measures against states that support terrorism. Other groupings of the industrialized democracies are obstructed either by mandate—NATO and the Organization for Economic Cooperation and Development (OECD), for example—or by geographical limitations on membership—the EC and the COE—from offering an adequate forum for U.S. policy on this issue.[2] Thus Washington has turned to the Summit Seven, almost by default, as a structure within which to work out collective measures.

25

The most salient feature of the Summit Seven group is that it is not formally an organization at all. It has no constitution, no written rules, and no permanent staff. In simplest terms, the leaders of the world's seven largest industrialized democratic states—Canada, West Germany, France, Italy, Japan, the United Kingdom, and the United States—have come to observe a tradition of gathering every year to discuss issues of mutual concern. The tradition originated in 1975, when the leaders of the Seven met at Rambouillet on the initiative of French President Valéry Giscard d'Estaing. The catalyst for the first summit gathering was the perceived need for some form of effective, top-level international meeting to address critical financial and economic problems in an informal, discreet setting.[3] But the summit meetings rather quickly became regularized by the annual rotation of the host government, the development of formal agendas, the holding of periodic preparatory meetings, and the issuance of joint concluding statements. By 1977, as one observer has put it, "the 'fireside era' was . . . definitively over."[4]

The purely economic agenda of the original Summit Seven concept lasted little longer than its vision of an informal ambience. The 1978 meeting saw the first public foray of the Seven governments into political issues with the Bonn Anti-Hijacking Declaration, which initiated Summit Seven counterterrorism cooperation. The Bonn Declaration emerged spontaneously from informal discussions among the leaders themselves during the summit meeting.[5] Despite this almost accidental beginning, every summit meeting thereafter would address sensitive political issues, frequently including international terrorism. By the fall of 1987, there would be six more summit declarations on international terrorism: Tokyo in 1979, Venice in 1980, Ottawa in 1981, London in 1984, Tokyo in 1986, and Venice in 1987. This chapter analyzes these declarations as they relate to the main categories of international terrorism.

Aviation Terrorism

By the mid-1970s, it had become evident that UN bodies such as ICAO or the General Assembly were not going to agree upon measures to put teeth into the potentially useful legal frameworks available to address the problem of aviation terrorism. And as long as states bent on harboring hijackers were free to do so without fear of consequences, the counterterrorism structures set up in the Hague and Montreal Conventions would remain fine legal formulas without much practical effect. The Seven addressed this enforcement gap in their first foray into the issue of terrorism in Bonn in 1978. And indeed, unlawful interference with international civil aviation has remained the most prominent concern of the Summit Seven governments in their statements on international terrorism: each of their declarations on terrorism has referred to this problem, either centrally or in passing.

The initial declaration of the Seven on terrorism, issued at the Bonn meeting in 1978, set the pattern.[6] It began by declaring the intention of the heads of state and government to "intensify their joint efforts to combat international terrorism." The one "joint effort" specifically identified in the declaration was the threat to impose an aviation boycott against any country that "refuses extradition or prosecution of those who have hijacked an aircraft and/or do [sic] not return such aircraft."

Whether they meant to or not, the seven heads of state and government assembled in Bonn hewed to a fairly subtle, and rather important, legal line in their terrorism declaration. Although it was clearly the Hague Convention obligations that the declaration was intended to support (the concept of mandatory extradition or prosecution of hijackers was derived from that convention), the declaration was not explicitly linked to the convention and in fact did not even mention it. To tie the sanctions of the declaration to formal violation of the Hague Convention, rather than to the actual refusal to extradite or prosecute the hijacker, would have meant that a country could evade the sanctions by the simple expedient of not signing the convention, thus avoiding its obligations altogether. The practical importance of this lay in the fact that some of the most prominent potential candidates for sanctions, including Cuba and Algeria, had not (and as of the fall of 1987 still had not) become parties to the Hague Convention. Further, such a link would have made the Bonn Declaration that much harder to use; the decision to apply it would have had to turn on whether the precise legal circumstances in a particular case constituted a violation of an international convention, rather than on the simple fact of a refusal to extradite or prosecute.

The relative informality of the declaration did have its disadvantage in the vagueness of its guidelines, a problem that groups of experts from the seven countries would later try to work out. But given all of the possible obstacles to effective use of the declaration, avoiding the addition of another layer of potential legal controversy was wise. Key international obligations embodied in the Hague Convention finally had an enforcement mechanism – but one technically separate from the convention framework itself.

What was the context of the Bonn Declaration? Skyjackings had actually peaked in number eight years before the declaration. In 1970, nearly 100 skyjackings were recorded, of which almost one-fifth were "terrorist" in nature. Between 1970 and 1978 the annual rate of skyjackings, "terrorist" and otherwise, had declined by more than half. Although there had been a sharp rise from 1976 to 1977, the year just before the Bonn Declaration, the total number of skyjackings in 1977 was fewer than 40, and of those not more than one-fifth was "terrorist."[7]

Despite the drop in overall occurrences, however, by the late 1970s skyjackings could hardly be said to have disappeared from the scene. During the five years 1973–1977, skyjackings occurred at an average rate of almost three a month.[8] The airlines of three of the Summit Seven countries – the United States, the United Kingdom, and West

Germany – had been among the most frequent victims.[9] In addition, two of the most sensational skyjackings in the months preceding the Bonn Declaration – a Japan Airlines hijacking by Japanese Red Army members in India in September 1977 and a Lufthansa hijacking in the Mediterranean in October 1977, in which the West German pilot was killed by the Arab hijackers – had involved aircraft of Summit Seven participants.[10] Not surprisingly, the problem of unlawful interference with international civil aviation would be on the minds of the leaders assembled in Bonn.

The United States hailed the Bonn Declaration. President Jimmy Carter said at the conclusion of the summit meeting:

> I personally believe that the strong statement on controlling air piracy, terrorism, is in itself worth the entire preparation and conduct of the summit. We are determined that this commitment be carried out individually and collectively. And our Foreign Ministers have been instructed immediately to contact other nations around the world without delay, to encourage them to join in with us in this substantive and, I think, adequate move to prevent air hijacking in the future.[11]

And in a statement issued shortly after the summit, the U.S. government reaffirmed its commitment to the declaration, calling it "a major advance in our efforts to combat aircraft hijacking" and noting that "[t]he seven summit participants are the major aviation powers of the free world; their airlines carry two-thirds of the free world passengers."[12]

Following the 1978 Bonn meeting, the U.S. government, in the first public notice of what would become a regular, if discreet, feature of Summit Seven counterterrorism work, stated: "As host government for the summit meeting, the German Government has convened a meeting of experts in Bonn . . . to develop specific procedures under the initiative of the Bonn declaration to deter air hijackings."[13] West Germany issued a report on the results of this meeting of experts:

> At the invitation of the Government of the Federal Republic of Germany, representatives of the seven Governments that participated in the Bonn Summit met in Bonn on August 1st and 2nd to discuss the practical implementation of the July 17th Bonn Declaration on hijacking. They agreed on a procedure to be followed under the Bonn Declaration in the case of a hijacking. They also discussed other issues related to the prompt implementation of the Declaration including ways of ensuring the widest possible international support for the initiative.[14]

The need for such discussions of "practical implementation" was unmistakable. First, the Bonn Declaration itself — as a statement worked out quickly and informally by heads of state and government — lacked sufficient guidelines for its own implementation. Some reduction of its sweeping language to operational detail was necessary if it was ever to be useful. What, for example, would constitute "refusal" to extradite or prosecute? What, for that matter, would constitute satisfactory extradition or prosecution? What would the offense of hijacking itself consist of for purposes of the declaration? How, operationally speaking, would the Seven make and implement the decision to apply the declaration to a particular country?

Second, above and beyond these procedural questions, any application of the sanctions envisioned in the declaration would pose thorny legal issues. Of particular potential difficulty was the question of how to square suspension of incoming flights from a target country with preexisting obligations under a bilateral civil aviation agreement giving that country's airlines the right to conduct such flights. Was the target country's harboring of hijackers in itself a sufficient legal reason to override existing agreements and suspend flights of that country's airlines? Or would Bonn Declaration adherents have to wait until such agreements expired before imposing sanctions? (As described below, in the one application of the Bonn Declaration so far—the case involving Ariana Afghan Airlines—the more conservative approach was taken: sanctions were imposed only after existing bilateral civil aviation agreements between Afghanistan and the states imposing the sanctions had expired.) The mandate of the "experts' group" was to provide answers to questions such as these.

The Seven returned to the subject of air hijacking at their 1979 meeting in Tokyo, indicating their "pleasure with the broad support expressed by other states" for the Bonn Declaration, mentioning agreement on procedures to implement that declaration (these procedures had been worked out at experts' meetings in London before the Tokyo summit), and "noting with satisfaction the widespread adherence to the conventions dealing with unlawful interference with civil aviation."[15] The Bonn Declaration was again reviewed by the Seven on a positive note the next year at their Venice meeting. The participants "expressed their satisfaction at the broad support of the international community for the principles set out in the Bonn declaration . . . as well as in the international conventions dealing with unlawful interference with civil aviation," and noted "the increasing adherence to these conventions and the responsible attitude taken by states with respect to air-hijacking." This optimism was tempered by the statement that "hijacking remains a threat to international civil aviation . . . there can be no relaxation of efforts to combat this threat."[16]

Statistically, the incidence of skyjackings, "terrorist" and otherwise, had remained roughly level in the two years since the Bonn Declaration, although there had been encouraging trends in the amount of support expressed by non-summit countries for the declaration itself as well as in the number of new parties to the Hague and Montreal Conventions.[17] But once again, airliners of Summit Seven countries—in this case, the United States and Italy—had been the targets of prominent terrorist hijackings in the months prior to the summit: in June 1979 an American Airlines jet was hijacked in the United States by a Serbian nationalist and flown to Ireland; and in September 1979 an Alitalia plane was hijacked in the Middle East by Lebanese Shi'as.[18]

The Ottawa Declaration issued at the following year's summit meeting took a very different tone. In this statement the Seven indicated "particular concern" over "recent hijacking incidents which threatened the safety of international civil aviation" and noted "several hijackings which have not been resolved by certain states in conformity with their obligations under international law."[19] The most notorious of the incidents to which this referred was the March 1981 hijacking of a Pakistani International Airlines domestic flight to Kabul, Afghanistan by Pakistani dissidents. This hijacking and the manner in which it had reportedly been handled by the Afghan authorities appeared to the summit participants to be an appropriate occasion to apply the sanctions envisaged in the Bonn Declaration three years earlier. Thus at Ottawa the Seven announced their intention "to suspend all flights to and from Afghanistan in implementation of the Bonn Declaration unless Afghanistan immediately takes steps to comply with its obligations."[20]

The Seven's statement at the 1984 London summit meeting returned to a more optimistic tone regarding air terrorism. In the London Declaration the heads of state and government noted that "hijacking . . . had declined since the Declarations of Bonn (1978), Venice (1980), and Ottawa (1981) as a result of improved security measures. . . . " Instead, newer forms of terrorism now merited the urgent attention of the Seven.[21]

Although the overall annual rate of hijackings in 1982 and 1983 remained very close to what it had been for the previous nine years, the number of "terrorist" hijackings dropped to a mere two incidents in 1983; in the first five months of 1984, the period just prior to the London summit, there were only eight hijackings in all.[22] Not only did this represent a rate well below that of previous years, but of these eight only one appeared to be "terrorist." Further, fewer and fewer hijackers were getting away; in the eight hijackings between January and May 1984, all the hijackers were taken into custody by responsible authorities immediately after each incident.[23] Thus, at the time there did appear to be some basis for the guarded optimism expressed in the London Declaration regarding aviation terrorism. In fact, later in the year President Reagan was to refer to international cooperation against air terrorism as an effort that had already achieved success: " . . . when we banded together we pretty much resolved the whole problem of skyjackings sometime ago."[24]

This relatively favorable picture was soon to change drastically. The period between the June 1984 London summit and the May 1986 Tokyo summit would witness a series of terrorist skyjacking spectaculars, most directed at airlines or nationals of Summit Seven countries and most ending with the hijackers eluding justice. These events included the July 1984 hijacking of an Air France plane to Tehran; the December 1984 hijacking of a Kuwaiti Airlines jet to Tehran, during which two U.S. nationals were murdered; the June 1985 hijacking of a TWA flight ending in Beirut, in the course of which one U.S. passenger was murdered and 39 passengers and crew members were held hostage in Beirut for 17 days; and the hijacking of an Egyptair jetliner to Malta in November 1985, during which the hijackers singled out and shot several U.S. (as well as Israeli) passengers.[25]

The 1986 Tokyo summit declaration on terrorism, however, which was issued only three weeks after the U.S. raid on Libya and focused largely on the problem of Libyan support of terrorism, referred only briefly to terrorist attacks on civil aviation. It is noteworthy in this context, however, because it was the first time the Seven expanded their attention to aircraft sabotage, though only implicitly: "We agree to make the 1978 Bonn Declaration more effective in dealing with *all forms* of terrorism affecting civil aviation."[26]

Although aircraft sabotage, like hijacking, was the subject of an international treaty concluded in the early 1970s, the Seven had never given it public attention before 1986. Sabotage is not only much rarer than hijacking but, because the sabotage incident is inherently brief, is usually less of a media spectacle when it does occur. Unlike hijackings, moreover, there are no visible perpetrators to be dealt with at the conclusion of such an incident.[27] Nonetheless, a few particularly horrifying sabotage incidents in the months preceding the Tokyo summit evidently helped to push this issue onto the summit's terrorism agenda: the possibly linked June 23, 1985 bombings of an Air India plane over the North Atlantic (in which all 329 passengers and crew were killed) and a CPAir (Canadian) plane just landed in Tokyo (in which two baggage handlers died), as well as the April 1986 explosion aboard a TWA flight over the Mediterranean that killed four U.S. passengers.[28]

Air terrorism returned to greater prominence in the 1987 Venice Declaration. Although the rate of attacks had fallen notably since the Tokyo Declaration of the year before, there had been one major terrorist incident directed against an aircraft of a Summit Seven country—the attack on a Pan American jetliner in Karachi, Pakistan in September 1986 by Arab extremists, which resulted in the death of 21 people and the wounding of more than 100.[29] Fulfilling the promise of the 1986 Tokyo Declaration, however, the Seven took a significant further step, on the basis of careful staff preparation, in constructing a framework for joint action against air terrorism. Pledging to continue their "efforts to improve the safety of travelers," they announced new measures "to make the 1978 Bonn Declaration more effective in dealing with all forms of terrorism affecting civil aviation."

The new measures, set forth in an annex to the main terrorism declaration, in effect extended the terms of the Bonn Declaration beyond aircraft hijacking to aircraft sabotage. The Seven agreed to impose Bonn Declaration sanctions against any country that refused to extradite or prosecute those who have committed "offenses described in the

Montreal Convention for the Suppression of Unlawful Acts against the Safety of Civil Aviation." They also announced their intention "in due time" to extend the Bonn Declaration "to cover any future amendment to the above convention or any other aviation conventions relating to the extradition or prosecution of the offenders."[30] It is unclear what the practical effect of this extension of the Bonn Declaration will be, however, since to date there have been no known cases in which a government has refused to prosecute or extradite a positively identified air sabotage suspect.

In the 1987 Venice Declaration the Seven maintained the position of the 1978 Bonn Declaration, avoiding a direct legal link between the imposition of sanctions and actual violation of the relevant convention. The convention in question is mentioned by name (unlike the Bonn Declaration), but only to define the range of terrorist offenses covered, not to establish violation of the Montreal Convention per se as the trigger for sanctions. The trigger remains the simple refusal to extradite or prosecute; only the range of offenses for which refusal will trigger sanctions has been expanded. The categories of offenses covered in the Montreal Convention, which are usually subsumed under the term "aircraft sabotage," are actually considerably more complex than the Hague Convention offenses, which can without significant distortion be covered by the simple term "hijacking." Rather than spell out the several subparagraphs of description of the offenses in the Montreal Convention, therefore, the Seven simply incorporated the description by reference.

Attacks on Internationally Protected Persons and Hostage-Taking

The Summit Seven have identified hostage-taking as a key area of concern from the time they first began to focus on international terrorism in 1978. The opening sentence of the Bonn Declaration stated the participants' concern over "terrorism and the taking of hostages," though the operational portion of the declaration was concerned solely with aircraft hijacking.[31] Terrorist seizures of hostages had been a prevalent phenomenon on the international scene since the beginning of the 1970s, averaging over 40 incidents a year from 1970 to 1978 and involving predominantly U.S. and West European victims.[32] The period before the Bonn summit meeting in July 1978 witnessed several major hostage-taking incidents, including the March 1978 seizure by South Moluccans of a government building with 71 employees in the Netherlands and the abduction and murder of industrialist Hans-Martin Schleyer by Red Army Faction members in West Germany in September 1977.[33]

The rate of hostage-takings did not abate in the period following the Bonn meeting, and at Venice in 1980 the Seven again addressed this problem, this time with a focus on diplomatic hostages. In the 1980 Venice Declaration the Seven, "gravely concerned by recent incidents of terrorism involving the taking of hostages and attacks on diplomatic and consular premises and personnel," reaffirmed their "determination to deter and combat such acts" and resolved "to provide to one another's diplomatic and consular missions support and assistance in situations involving the seizure of diplomatic and consular establishments or personnel."[34] In their comments on the summit meeting, several leaders of the Seven, including President Giscard d'Estaing, President Carter, Prime Minister Margaret Thatcher, and Prime Minister Pierre Trudeau, referred positively to the terrorism declaration.[35]

The Seven's attention to this subject was amply justified by the pattern of international terrorism evident at the time of the Venice meeting. By 1980 diplomats had become, in the words of the State Department, "the major target of international terrorism."[36] In that year 54 percent of all international terrorist attacks, according to the department's figures, were directed against diplomats — a proportion that would remain roughly constant through 1983.[37] The number of international terrorist incidents involving foreign diplomats that resulted in casualties doubled from 1978 to 1980; the number of actual casualties more than doubled. For the two years 1979 and 1980 almost 400 persons were killed or wounded in international terrorist incidents involving foreign diplomats.[38] Summit Seven countries had a particular interest in this type of terrorism: by far the largest number of victims of terrorist attacks on diplomats were U.S. personnel, and Western Europe was the scene of more such attacks than any other major world region.[39]

The Venice meeting also was held in the shadow of several sensational terrorist incidents that involved diplomats of Summit Seven countries or took place in those countries' territory. In February 1979 U.S. Ambassador Adolph Dubs was seized by terrorists in Kabul and ultimately killed in a shoot-out between the kidnappers and Afghan security forces.[40] In March 1979 Irish Republican Army gunmen assassinated the UK ambassador to The Hague. In February 1980 the radical leftist M-19 group seized the Dominican embassy in Bogotá, Colombia, capturing, among others, ambassadors of 11 countries, including the U.S. ambassador, who was held along with 17 other hostages for two months.[41] In April 1980 the Iranian embassy in London was seized by Arabs from Iran; 26 hostages were taken, two of whom were killed by the terrorists a few days later. And as the heads of state and government were meeting in June 1980, 52 U.S. diplomatic personnel were still being held hostage in Tehran following the seizure of the U.S. embassy there by a mob of students in November 1979.[42]

But if the backdrop of the Venice Declaration on terrorism against diplomats was as compelling as that of the Bonn Declaration on air terrorism two years before, the process of its adoption was quite different. The 1978 Bonn meeting was the first at which the seven leaders, as a group, openly dealt with any purely political subject, and there had evidently been no joint staff preparation for the statement on hijacking. In contrast, only two years later the notion of the Seven jointly addressing political topics had become practically institutionalized, and the Venice Declaration on terrorism against diplomats, as well as the several other political declarations issued at that meeting, had been prepared before the summit by groups of officials of the Seven governments.[43] Other patterns that would characterize the Seven's counterterrorism activity were also emerging: it was the United States that took the lead in preparing and issuing the Venice Declaration, while France displayed the greatest reluctance to have the Seven address political matters, including terrorism, at all.[44]

Reflecting the continuing high rate of terrorist attacks on diplomats, the Ottawa Declaration of 1981 also devoted considerable attention to this problem. At Ottawa the Seven resolved that "any state which directly aids and abets the commission of terrorist acts condemned in the Venice statement should face a prompt international response." They also agreed to "explore cooperative measures for dealing with and countering acts of terrorism, for promoting more effective implementation of existing anti-terrorist conventions, and for securing wider adherence to them."

Diplomats remained a top target for terrorists in 1982 and 1983, and this problem continued to receive attention from the Seven. It was announced in January 1984 that security experts from the Seven governments had met in Washington "to discuss our continuing joint efforts to carry out the Venice Declaration of 1981 [sic] on protection of diplomatic personnel."[45] As it turned out, however, 1984 was the year the diplomatic community, now protected by substantial security improvements, became less attractive as a target for international terrorism. Less than one-fifth of the targets of international terrorist attacks that year were diplomatic.[46] At the London meeting in June, the Seven noted that the types of terrorism addressed in the Bonn, Venice, and Ottawa declarations had declined since those declarations had been issued, "as a result of improved security measures."[47] In fact, the London summit participants devoted their attention to a new terrorist threat: not that directed against diplomats, but that instigated by them.[48] And in the period following the summit, though terrorism against diplomats did not cease, it declined still further, accounting in 1985 for less than 10 percent of international terrorist incidents.[49] The 1986 Tokyo Declaration did not mention this form of terrorism at all.[50]

Through the early 1980s, it might have seemed that hostage-taking too was a diminishing problem. At London in 1984 the Seven noted a "decline" in hostage-taking in the years since the previous summit declarations. There was some truth to this, though like many such judgments it depended entirely on the period examined. Although the number of hostage incidents in 1984 was by far the lowest since 1970 – a mere 6 – in 1983 it was 75, actually the highest since figures began to be kept 15 years earlier.[51]

But even on the most favorable assumptions, the optimistic conclusion about hostage-taking reflected in the London Declaration was to be utterly refuted in 1985 – a year in which hostage-takers, led by Lebanese terrorists, broke all records with a total of 89 seizures.[52] The 1986 Tokyo Declaration, however, oriented as it was toward the problem of Libyan-sponsored terrorism, did not address hostage-taking specifically. But at Venice in 1987, against a backdrop of continued hostage incidents, the Seven again singled out this form of terrorism, along with aircraft hijacking, for special mention, although no specific measures relating to it were discussed in the summit terrorism statement.[53]

Terrorist Abuse of Diplomatic Immunities

Although diplomatic protection has been exploited for the planning and commission of politically motivated crimes for many centuries, terrorist abuse of diplomatic privileges and immunities did not become a prominent issue in modern counterterrorism until 1984, with the notorious incident of the shootings from the Libyan People's Bureau in London. The viciousness of the attack and the apparent immunity of those responsible from any form of legal process seemed to open a whole new era of vulnerability to terrorism—and one of great political sensitivity for leaders of major democratic countries.

Not surprisingly, the declaration on international terrorism issued at the summit meeting in June 1984, which happened to be held in London, was concerned primarily with this new type of terrorist threat. In that statement, the Seven "viewed with serious concern the increasing involvement of states and governments in acts of terrorism, including the abuse of diplomatic immunity." They "acknowledge[d] the inviolability of diplomatic missions and other requirements of international law; but they emphasized the obligations which that law also entails."

Among the "proposals which found support in the [summit] discussion," according to the London statement, were the "use of the powers of the receiving state under the Vienna Convention on Diplomatic Relations in such matters as the size of diplomatic missions, and the number of buildings enjoying diplomatic immunity"; "consultation and as far as possible cooperation over the expulsion or exclusion from their countries of known terrorists, including persons of diplomatic status involved in terrorism"; and "action by each country to review the sale of weapons to states supporting terrorism."

That there was a summit statement on terrorism at all was something of a victory for the governments that had looked for an affirmative stance on the issue, especially the United States and the United Kingdom, in the face of the traditional French reservations.[54] The British and U.S. governments praised the London Declaration, but, taking account of its rather cautious tone, restrained their enthusiasm. Foreign Secretary Geoffrey Howe noted the declaration's intent to "give impetus" to counterterrorism efforts.[55] Secretary of State Shultz said:

> Of course, private actions on something like this are the key. But there is a great deal of importance, I think, attached to identifying this problem publicly so people

can see that the heads of these governments assembled
felt that it was important enough to spend that much
time on and to develop it in the detail that it has been
developed in this statement. . . .
    . . . I'm simply delighted that in this meeting there
was this much attention to the subject, and the statement was as extensive and forward-looking as the one
that's been produced here. . . . Everyone is concerned
and wants to see things advance, but yet we don't want
to overstate or over-display our hand here.[56]

In September of that year a group of counterterrorism
experts from the Summit Seven governments met in London to examine practical measures related to the subject
matter of the London Declaration. Aside from the London
shooting, no government reported any recent instances of
terrorist abuse of diplomatic privileges and immunities.[57]
During the next two years, however, it would become evident that this was indeed a potentially serious problem. In
July 1985 a Jordanian diplomat was killed in Turkey; the
second secretary of the Syrian embassy was later indicted
in connection with the murder.[58] In March 1986 the German-Arab Friendship Union in West Berlin was bombed
with the logistical support, according to one of the defendants, of the Syrian embassy in East Berlin. In April 1986,
a plot to bomb an El Al jetliner leaving London was foiled;
the British government announced it had conclusive evidence of official Syrian involvement in this plot, carried out
largely through the Syrian embassy in London.[59] And also
in April 1986 a discotheque frequented by U.S. soldiers in
West Berlin was bombed; the U.S. government claimed it
had evidence that the attack had been directed by the Libyan embassy in East Berlin and, in response, launched an air
raid against Libya with the stated intention of disrupting
that country's capacity to plan and direct terrorist attacks
on U.S. facilities and nationals abroad.[60]
    In this light it is not surprising that state-supported
terrorism, as manifested largely through abuse of diplomat-

ic immunities, was the primary concern of the May 1986 Tokyo summit statement. Held just weeks after the highly controversial U.S. raid against Libya, the summit meeting could hardly avoid coming to grips with this issue. There were indications in the days before the meeting that key participants were prepared to take a strong common stand against state-supported terrorism in general and Libya in particular. Most important, a week before the Tokyo meeting, the French, who had distinctly lacked solidarity with the United States on the Libya raid just three weeks before, made it clear that they were now prepared to support a vigorous counterterrorism stance by the major Western countries. The French announcement was made after a meeting between the French and British prime ministers in the United Kingdom, implying some British influence on the French position.[61] The more forthcoming stand of rightwing Prime Minister Jacques Chirac on international counterterrorism cooperation, as compared with that of the previous Socialist government, was also cited as a factor in the French change of heart.[62]

The Tokyo Declaration lived up to expectations. The summit participants singled out for particular condemnation the "blatant and cynical use [of terrorism] as an instrument of government policy." In contrast to the understated language of the London Declaration of two years before, where proposals only "found support in the discussion," the leaders at Tokyo spoke in unequivocal declarative phrases: "We, the Heads of State or Government, agree to intensify the exchange of information"; "We specify the following as measures open to any government"; "We have decided to apply these measures"; "Each of us is committed"; "We will maintain close cooperation." Even more striking was the mention of a specific state, Libya, as being "clearly involved in sponsoring or supporting international terrorism."

The actual counterterrorism measures specified in the Tokyo statement included "refusal to export arms to states which sponsor or support terrorism"; "strict limits on the size of the diplomatic and consular missions and other official bodies abroad of states which engage in [terrorist] activities, control of travel of members of such missions and bodies, and, where appropriate, radical reductions in, or even the closure of, such missions and bodies"; and "denial of entry to all persons, including diplomatic personnel, who have been expelled or excluded from one of our states on suspicion of involvement in international terrorism or who have been convicted of a terrorist offence."

The Tokyo terrorism statement, the strongest of general application since the Bonn Declaration of 1978, was perceived as a vindication of the tougher U.S. and British positions and was hailed by the United States. Secretary of State Shultz declared:

> I think it's a terrific statement. I can't tell you how pleased I am at how strong this statement is. It is very good to come here after all this talk and turmoil and discussion and find how strongly everybody feels about the problem of terrorism, how ready people are to work on it, how totally nonexistent is any argument about Libya's complicity and how ready people are to isolate them. So I think it's wonderful.

The secretary also praised Prime Minister Thatcher, who reportedly provided the key impetus for the forcefulness of the final statement, calling her "a terrific leader" and remarking: "I can't imagine any way that we could give her more support; if somebody could point it out, we'd do it."[63]

Meanwhile the French, perhaps taken aback by their own boldness in signing such a forthright statement, quickly pointed out (along with the Japanese) that the summit declaration was discretionary only and that each nation was still free to decide for itself how to proceed in the fight against terrorism.[64]

Although new revelations of state involvement in terrorist acts continued to appear during the ensuing year—most strikingly in November 1986 when British courts concluded that the Syrian government had indeed been involved in attempting to place a bomb aboard an El Al plane leaving London in April of that year—nothing nearly as dramatic as the events of spring 1986 took place during this period. Statistics showed that the incidence of terrorism in general slowed considerably.[65] In fact, the period preceding the June 1987 summit meeting in Venice was noteworthy less for terrorist incidents than for developments in the world of counterterrorism.

Meetings of counterterrorism experts of the Seven governments had been held quietly at irregular intervals ever since the beginning of the group's work on the issue in 1978. But in 1987 such meetings became a public political issue for the first time. In early February the United States, against the backdrop of a major naval buildup in the eastern Mediterranean, proposed (with Italian support) a meeting of counterterrorism officials of the Seven governments in Rome to discuss the Lebanese hostage situation. But several other members of the Seven declined to meet, cautioning the United States against any military action aimed at terrorist bases in Lebanon.[66]

The French Foreign Ministry, announcing that a counterterrorism gathering had been proposed by Italy and the United States, said that the proposed meeting "aroused objections concerning its nature and timing" and stated that "bilateral actions are more profitable concerning the hostages problem." The French cautioned that it would be "dangerous for the Seven to appear as the world's gendarmes, especially in the current context," asserting that Great Britain and West Germany "fully share the French Government's opinion."[67] The reluctance of the West German government reportedly was caused by concerns for the safety of two German businessmen recently taken hostage in Lebanon.[68] Objections also were reported from the British government, concerned in particular about the fate of Church of England envoy Terry Waite, who had been taken hostage January 20.

In response to these objections the United States withdrew its proposal for the meeting. The following day Washington reduced its armada off Lebanon, a move seen as designed largely to provide reassurance to the allies about U.S. intentions.[69] Evidently the spirit of the Tokyo Declaration did not apply to the more ambiguous and very sensitive situation of the Western hostages in Lebanon, where the French, Germans, and British appeared to feel that quiet and patient bilateral tactics were at least safer, if not more effective, than public displays of allied solidarity.

Only a few months later, however, on May 28, the impression left by the aborted Rome meeting was somewhat dispelled by a meeting in Paris of senior counterterrorism officials of the Seven governments, along with representatives of Belgium and Denmark, who were, respectively, the current and future EC presidents. The purpose of the gathering, according to French Interior Minister Charles Pasqua, was "to stimulate intelligence-sharing and other assistance among the industralized world's police and intelligence agencies fighting terrorism."[70]

Although no concrete results were announced, the meeting was significant for at least two reasons. First, it was at the cabinet level. Most governments sent their interior ministers; Attorney General Edwin Meese attended for the United States. This was a sharp contrast to all previous meetings of Seven counterterrorism experts, which had been at a considerably lower level. The resulting prominence of the meeting was a new phenomenon in Western counterterrorism efforts. Second, it had been organized, and rather suddenly at that, by the French (with some help from the Germans), who historically – and as recently as the February impasse over the proposed meeting in Rome – had been firmly opposed to any expansion of the Seven's work in this area. It was open to question whether this new role represented so much a change in "official" French policy as it did a difference in approach between the more traditionalist Foreign Ministry, with the usual responsibility for Summit Seven counterterrorism work, and the more pragmatic Interior Ministry, which had been in charge of organizing the May meeting.[71] Political as well as bureaucratic rivalries within the French government may have played a role too.[72] But what was clear, and probably more important in any event, was that the meeting, coming on the heels of French counterterrorism agreements with Germany, Italy, and most recently Spain, and on the eve of the Venice summit, gave the strongest possible signal of a new French willingness to cooperate openly with other Western democracies in the political campaign against international terrorism.

The United States, characterizing the meeting as but the first in a series, expressed satisfaction. Attorney General Meese called it "a very important first step" and an "excellent idea."[73] "The trend is going in the right direction," commented State Department counterterrorism head Bremer.[74] The French themselves were careful not to overplay its significance, and Interior Minister Pasqua cautioned: "No one has proposed the creation of a new institution, a new bureaucracy, a new system in the anti-terrorist struggle. What we lack is a sort of political or ministerial link in regard to the anti-terrorist struggle."[75]

The timing of the Paris meeting, its lack of specific subject matter or announced results, and the haste with which it had been organized aroused speculation that its real goal was to create a more activist atmosphere at the Venice summit. Indeed, the Paris meeting was openly portrayed as advance work: British Home Secretary Douglas Hurd, for example, called the Paris discussions "a good preparation for the Venice summit."[76]

The Venice terrorism statement of June 1987, however, essentially reaffirmed past summit declarations, making an effort at modest progress in one specific area—aircraft sabotage. Stylistically, it lacked the steely resonance of its Tokyo predecessor; on the issue of state involvement in terrorism, it declared merely that the Seven "remain resolved to apply, in respect of any state clearly involved in sponsoring or supporting international terrorism, effective measures within the framework of international law and in our own jurisdictions." It did nod in the direction of the Paris counterterrorism meeting, but fell somewhat short of enthusiastic endorsement, with the leaders declaring: "[We] welcome the progress made in international cooperation against terrorism since we last met in Tokyo in May 1986, and in particular the initiative taken by France and Germany to convene in Paris a meeting of ministers of nine countries, who are responsible for counter-terrorism." Their statement also confirmed "the commitment of each of us to the principle of making no concessions to terrorists or their sponsors."[77]

Not only the lack of recent dramatic events in the world of terrorism, but also the unusually difficult political preoccupations of most of the leaders assembled in Venice – President Reagan's Iran-contra scandal, Prime Minister Thatcher's imminent elections, the Italian government's role as caretaker, France's split political personality, Japanese Prime Minister Yasuhiro Nakasone's severe domestic weaknesses – may have contributed to the relatively subdued nature of the Venice statement. But it would not be appropriate to make too much, as some U.S. media commentators did, of the so-called tepid nature of the declaration.[78] Its tone was certainly less bold than that of the previous year, but in historical perspective it was no less forceful than the average of its five predecessors. Moreover, the substantive advance reflected in its annex on aircraft sabotage, though modest, was as real as any in previous summit statements.

Secretary of State Shultz characterized the statement as reflecting increasing counterterrorism cooperation among the summit nations. "We see more and more emphasis – no concessions, no place to hide," the secretary said. "States sponsoring terrorism can expect trouble from us."[79]

3

Cooperation in Action:
Selected Terrorist Incidents
and the Western Response

This chapter examines the response of the major Western democracies to six selected terrorist incidents. The selection of these cases was based on certain guidelines. First, these incidents offer a cross-section of types of terrorist behavior—hijacking, hostage-taking, abuse of diplomatic immunities, shootings, and bombings—and of types of responses—economic, political, military, and law enforcement. Second, they represent a varied and realistic picture of counterterrorism successes and failures. Third, the incidents all have a strong element of state involvement, ranging from passive acquiescence to active planning and support. And finally and most important, for one reason or another the question of a Western collective response was a prominent consideration in all of them.

The PIA Hijacking

On March 2, 1981 the government of Pakistan announced that a Pakistan International Airlines (PIA) jet on a domestic flight from Karachi to Peshawar had been hijacked to Kabul, Afghanistan by Pakistani political dissidents demanding the release of "political prisoners" held in Paki-

stani prisons.[1] Negotiations between the hijackers, who were holding the seized aircraft with 115 hostages aboard, and authorities on the ground in Kabul (including a Pakistani delegation) were still under way five days later when the hijackers shot and killed a Pakistani diplomat who had been a passenger.[2] Two days later the hijacked aircraft, with the three hijackers and more than 100 hostages aboard, was flown to Damascus, Syria, where negotiations continued.[3] On March 12 the hijacking ended peacefully in Damascus, with Pakistan agreeing to free all 55 "political prisoners" demanded by the hijackers and the latter freeing all hostages aboard the seized jet.[4] As part of the deal that ended the hijacking, Syria, at the request of the Pakistani government, agreed to provide temporary asylum to the hijackers and to receive the prisoners being released from Pakistani prisons.[5]

This hijacking spawned bitter accusations, denials, and counteraccusations by the two states most directly involved as well as by the two superpowers. Five days into the incident the U.S. government charged that the Soviets had so far made "no apparent effort" to resolve the situation and called upon them to "use their influence in Kabul to achieve an early release of the passengers and crew and a peaceful end to the incident."[6] The Soviet Union labeled the U.S. statement "absurd," defending the actions of the Afghan authorities in handling the hijacking and accusing the Pakistani authorities of "delaying, manoeuvring, [and] marking time."[7]

The Afghan government released the contents of a message it had sent to UN Secretary General Kurt Waldheim, asserting that "the Democratic Republic of Afghanistan, in conformity with the international civil aviation convention and the responsibilities emanating from it, has made unreserved efforts to maintain the safety and life of the passengers and crews on board the Pakistani hijacked plane at the Kabul international airport and to obtain their release." The message further declared that Afghanistan would "hold the government of Pakistan fully responsible for its delaying

tactics if the lives of the passengers and the crews on board are endangered."[8]

Meanwhile, a senior Pakistani official charged that the hijackers in Kabul had been provided with "all sorts of facilities from the outside." He remarked pointedly that "this was the first instance in the history of hijacking that the hijackers were still active and energetic both physically and mentally even seven days after a hijacking" and that "it is also amazing that three [hijackers] are managing to keep a constant watch on 115 people without any help."[9]

Afghanistan responded heatedly to Pakistani allegations of complicity with the hijackers. The Afghan government declared that it "resolutely rejects the allegations that the Kabul authorities have links with the hijackers" and added: "It must be stated decisively that all responsibility concerning the hijacking of the plane rests in every way upon the shoulders of the government of Pakistan and its relevant authorities. These authorities, ignoring the civil aviation regulations, did not take appropriate measures to prevent the hijackers boarding the plane with weapons and explosives."[10]

But Pakistan reiterated and intensified its accusations following the conclusion of the hijacking. President Mohammed Zia ul-Haq alleged that there was a "deep conspiracy" between the Kabul regime and Pakistani dissidents and that the Afghans had provided the hijackers with weapons.[11] And the United States renewed its complaints about Soviet behavior in connection with the hijacking. A State Department spokesman said: "I don't see how the Soviets can entirely escape responsibility for what took place." The United States also charged that the hijackers had been given weapons while on the ground in Kabul.[12] The Soviets rejected the charges, accusing the U.S. government of trying to "make propaganda mileage out of this human tragedy."[13]

Late the following month the hijackers reportedly went to Kabul.[14] Shortly thereafter Pakistan made a formal demand, citing the Hague and Montreal Conventions, that

Afghanistan "hand over to it immediately and unconditionally the three Pakistani hijackers."[15] Afghanistan did not hand over the hijackers, but a few weeks later Pakistani authorities announced that they had apprehended one of the three hijackers near the Pakistani-Afghan border.[16]

These, then, were the circumstances the Summit Seven governments had before them in considering the application of Bonn Declaration sanctions against the Afghan airline, Ariana, at the Ottawa summit meeting in July 1981: two of the three hijackers of the PIA aircraft were still residing in Afghanistan despite a formal Pakistani request for their extradition, and there were strong lingering overtones of Afghan (and Soviet) abetment of the hijacking itself. Against such a backdrop the Seven issued this statement:

> The Heads of State and Government are convinced that, in the case of the hijacking of a Pakistan International Airlines aircraft in March, the conduct of the Babrak Karmal government of Afghanistan, both during the incident and subsequently in giving refuge to the hijackers, was and is in flagrant breach of its international obligations under the Hague Convention to which Afghanistan is a party, and constitutes a serious threat to air safety. Consequently the Heads of State and Government propose to suspend all flights to and from Afghanistan in implementation of the Bonn Declaration unless Afghanistan immediately takes steps to comply with its obligations. Furthermore, they call up on all states which share their concern for air safety to take appropriate action to persuade Afghanistan to honor its obligations.

It is notable that in this statement the Seven failed to maintain the position reflected in the Bonn Declaration itself of preserving the nominal independence of the Bonn sanctions process from the Hague Convention. Given the legal uncertainties accompanying this maiden collective effort to cut off aviation to a country accused of harboring hijackers, the Seven opted to play it safe and use the strongest possible legal position – one based on an explicit assertion of actual violations of an international convention. Rather than the original Bonn formula of simple refusal to extradite or prosecute accused hijackers, therefore, the sanctions were directly linked to alleged Afghan violations of the Hague Convention. In this case it made no real difference because Afghanistan happens to be a party to the Hague Convention, but it would be unfortunate if the position of formal independence from the convention established in the Bonn Declaration were undermined.

The action threatened at the Ottawa summit was implemented on November 30, 1981 when the following statement was issued:

> The Heads of State and Government of the seven economic Summit countries declared at Ottawa on July 20, 1981 that they proposed to suspend all flights to and from Afghanistan in implementation of the Bonn Declaration unless the Babrak Karmal regime took immediate steps to comply with Afghanistan's international obligations by extraditing or prosecuting under the Hague Convention the hijackers of the PIA aircraft. The statement of the seven was communicated to the Mission of Afghanistan to the United Nations by Canada on behalf of the seven. Since no reply has been received from the Kabul regime, France, the FRG and the UK, which are the only countries among the seven to whose territories Ariana Afghan Airlines fly, have decided in agreement with the other members of the Seven to denounce their air services agreements or arrangements with Afghanistan. Notice to this effect will be given.[17]

The Afghan government did, however, eventually respond to the Seven at the UN. In a note delivered to the UN missions of the Summit Seven states on October 28, 1982, the Afghan mission stated:

The Government, according to the decision of the
Council of Ministers of the Democratic Republic of Afghanistan, and in compliance with and honor of its
international obligation with regards to hijackers,
assures that whenever the hijackers of Pakistan
International Airlines enter Afghanistan, they will be
arrested and prosecuted.

Therefore, on the basis of the foregoing under-
takings, the Democratic Republic of Afghanistan
respectfully requests that all sanctions imposed or
contemplated against it and its national airline be
terminated.[18]

This Afghan submission, implicitly claiming that the hijackers were no longer in Afghanistan and that consequently no legal action could be undertaken by Afghan authorities against them, did not cause the Seven to relent. Civil
aviation links between Afghanistan and the Seven were du-
ly terminated in accordance with the November 30, 1981
statement after the notice of termination periods in the
relevant bilateral agreements had elapsed. Shortly before
the severance, Ariana approached several other West European countries in an attempt to obtain alternative traffic
rights, but no such rights were granted, and Ariana flights
to Western Europe ceased entirely.[19]

In early December 1982 the president of Ariana condemned the boycott, claiming that Afghanistan had re-
spected its international commitments in connection with
the PIA hijacking and had so informed the Seven. He expressed the hope that the Seven would review their decision
"because Afghanistan is a landlocked country and therefore
no international regulations allow the closure of international civil air spaces and their airports to the flights of its
aeroplanes." He complained (not without some basis) that
many other incidents of hijacking had taken place without
ensuing sanctions being applied against any involved
countries.[20]

In mid-1984 Kabul Radio reported that one of the three
PIA hijackers had been executed in Kabul on a conviction

of murder unrelated to the PIA hijacking.[21] The report, if true (it was disputed by Afghan exiles in Pakistan), would indicate that only one of the three PIA hijackers remained alive and at large at that time. In any event, the Bonn Declaration sanctions remained in effect until 1986, when the Seven, evidently concluding that they had achieved their purpose, quietly ended them.[22]

The success of the Ariana case in terms of collective action against international terrorism was real. The Summit Seven governments did just what they had undertaken to do—suspended flights to and from a country that harbored aircraft hijackers. At the same time, however, this case demonstrated the difficulty of fitting counterterrorism enforcement into broader international political concerns. The Seven's response to the hijacking—as reflected so clearly in U.S. accusations of Soviet complicity in the incident itself—could not be divorced from broader East-West tensions stemming from the Soviet invasion and occupation of Afghanistan. If the country that had given sanctuary to hijackers had been governed by a pro-Western regime (perhaps dependent upon Western aid to stave off a Communist insurgency) instead of a Marxist regime installed by Soviet forces, it is difficult to believe that the Summit Seven response would have been as strong.

The effort to enforce an international norm against hijacking suffers to the extent that such an effort is affected by extraneous political considerations. Such considerations of course inevitably intrude, and it is useless to pretend that counterterrorism enforcement can be handled as only a matter of upholding established international norms. For example, one of the key concerns—and a legitimate one—of the Summit Seven governments in considering the lifting of sanctions against Ariana was undoubtedly to avoid even a slight appearance of signaling tacit approval of the overall political situation in Afghanistan. But such outside concerns must be thought through in advance as much as possible to minimize the risk that, through inertia or intention, they will dominate the counterterrorism initiative to the detriment of overall counterterrorism policy. From this perspective the Ariana sanctions were not a positive precedent.

The Air India Hijacking

On November 25, 1981 a band of armed mercenaries attacked the international airport near Victoria, the capital of the Seychelles, in an apparent effort to overthrow the Seychelles government. The assault was unsuccessful, and to make their escape the attackers commandeered an Air India jetliner that had landed during the fighting for a refueling stop on its way from Bombay to Harare, Zimbabwe. They ordered the jet, with 65 passengers and 14 crew aboard, to fly to South Africa. Upon landing in Durban, the passengers and crew were released unharmed, and the 44 mercenaries who had commandeered the plane—a mixed group of South Africans, Zimbabweans, Britons, Americans, and others—were taken into custody by South African authorities.[23]

There were conflicting reports of South African involvement in or knowledge of the coup attempt, but the South African government strongly denied any involvement, stating that it had been approached several times by Seychelles dissidents for help with such plans but had refused.[24] A few days later the South African authorities released without charges 39 of the 44 hijackers. The remaining 5 were charged with kidnapping and released on bail. No charges related to the hijacking itself were filed.[25] The South African minister of police commented: "They only shot out some windows and ran around in the bush. You tell me what law they broke in South Africa."[26]

Reaction from the U.S. government was stiff. On December 2 the State Department requested "prompt and severe punishment" for those involved and noted: "South Africa is a party to the Hague Convention against hijacking, which obligates the government of South Africa to submit for prosecution or extradite persons accused of unlawfully seizing aircraft. The United States has made its views of this issue known to the South African government."[27] The following day the State Department spokesman reported that the United States was "consulting with the Bonn Summit Declaration countries on the applicability of the Declaration in this instance."[28] In Britain, influential political voices accused the South Africans of violating the Hague Convention and called publicly for cessation of flights to and from South Africa.[29] Privately the British and U.S. governments made it known to South Africa that if proper law enforcement measures were not taken against the hijackers, there was a real possibility that Bonn Declaration sanctions would be invoked.[30]

In the face of this pressure the South African stance began to change. By December 6 the South African authorities let it be known that the 44 mercenaries could still be charged with hijacking.[31] Within the month all 44 were in fact charged with civil aviation offenses related to the hijacking.[32] Trials were held in the spring of 1982; 42 of the defendants were found guilty on July 27 and sentenced to various prison terms ranging from 5 to 30 years.[33]

Thus 1981 had been a year of promise for the Summit Seven effort to construct an international mechanism to suppress air terrorism by punishing countries that harbored hijackers. In the case of Afghanistan, invoking sanctions demonstrated the viability and credibility of the Bonn Declaration, even though the results were unclear and even though the background of East-West rivalry over Afghanistan undermined the Seven's claim to impartial enforcement of international norms. In the case of South Africa, the mere threat of invoking sanctions may have helped persuade the authorities to take the proper steps. Although a link cannot be proven, it is reasonable to assume that the very recent Afghan example was one factor the South African officials considered. This situation thus demonstrated the potential benefits of a show of will by the Summit Seven and like-minded states.

The TWA 847 Hijacking

Unfortunately, the promise inherent in Western handling of the two 1981 hijacking incidents was not to be fulfilled in the ensuing years. Of all the various cases, from 1982 until the fall of 1987, in which its application would have been in order, the Bonn Declaration was not applied once.[34] Although each hijacking case had its unique characteristics, perhaps the one that most clearly revealed the dubious condition of the Bonn Declaration in the mid-1980s was the hijacking of TWA 847.

This incident, which etched indelible images of terrorism into the minds of millions around the world and preempted policy-making attention in several capitals for more than two weeks, began on Friday, June 14, 1985 when two Lebanese Shi'as hijacked the TWA flight carrying 153 passengers and crew to Beirut shortly after takeoff from Athens en route to Rome. Over the next three days the hijackers, their numbers considerably augmented by Shi'a militiamen who boarded the aircraft in Beirut, ordered the plane flown back and forth between Algiers and Beirut on two successive round trips, in the process releasing all but 40 hostages. During the second stop in Beirut on June 15, the terrorists murdered U.S. Navy diver Robert Stethem. On Monday, June 17, after the plane had finally come to rest at Beirut, the remaining 39 hostages, all U.S. nationals, were removed to various locations in Beirut under guard of Shi'a militiamen.[35]

During the early days of the hijacking, the hijackers issued various demands that included release of all Arab detainees from Israeli prisons and complete Israeli withdrawal from Lebanese territory.[36] By June 17, however, when the hostages had been taken off the aircraft and Shi'a militia leader Nabih Berri had assumed some measure of control over the situation, the main demand had crystallized: the release of Lebanese detainees who had been removed from Lebanon by Israeli troops during Israel's withdrawal the previous year. The detainees, numbering some 700, were held in Atlit prison in Israel. This demand was explicitly adopted by Berri on behalf of his Amal movement, though the original hijackers were thought to be more closely connected with a different Lebanese Shi'a group, Hizballah.[37]

As the nominal government of Lebanon went through the motions of addressing the crisis while the real players pursued their business with almost total disregard of that government's actions, the implications of the situation began to emerge more fully. In the chaotic state of Lebanese politics, the local "authorities" — those political and security forces with an ability to control and influence the situation at the site of the hijacking — were operating on a set of assumptions completely different from those of the typical government faced with such a problem. To these authorities, the hijacking was not a criminal or security problem to be resolved as quickly as possible through the neutralization or apprehension of the hijackers and the safe release of the hostages. Rather, it was above all a political opportunity to be exploited through alliance with the hijackers and partial adoption of their demands, while presenting to the rest of the world an image of honest brokers and mediators trying to consider the interests of all "sides." Further complications arose from the fact that the chief demand of those in control of the TWA hostages was directed not against the U.S. government, whose nationals and flag aircraft had been seized, but against a third party — Israel.

Out of the next two weeks of labyrinthine public and private maneuvering involving the United States, Syria, Israel, Algeria, Amal, Hizballah, the Red Cross, and numerous other governments and parties in the Middle East and Europe, a resolution emerged. The TWA hostages would be released through Damascus. Israel would release in stages all the Atlit detainees, and Washington would state that "the United States reaffirms its longstanding support for the preservation of Lebanon, its Government, its stability, and its security, and for the mitigation of the suffering of its people."[38]

But some very troubling questions were left in the wake of the release of the U.S. hostages. How could the normal follow-up processes of apprehending and prosecuting the perpetrators be undertaken when the authorities formally responsible for such steps did not even have the capacity to conduct a routine criminal trial? How could these processes be set in motion in the first place when the original hijackers, even before the conclusion of the incident, had merged into a veritable crowd of accomplices and vanished into the terra incognita of West Beirut, where the government's authority ran very shallow indeed? Perhaps most unsettling of all, how could normal law enforcement measures against the hijackers even be contemplated when the man officially responsible for such measures, Lebanese Minister of Justice Nabih Berri, was himself arguably an accomplice to the hijacking? (As Secretary of State Shultz said at a press conference the evening the hostages were released, "I think we have some sorting out to do about Mr. Berri.")[39] Given these realities, what could justify, and what would be the point of, imposing sanctions against a government that clearly had practically no control over the situation in the first place? In short, how could all of the standard international antihijacking measures embodied in instruments like the Hague Convention and the Bonn Declaration be applied to the TWA 847 case?

In looking beyond the immediate goal of safe release of the hostages, U.S. attention first turned, even before the crisis was over, to the problem of Beirut International Airport itself. Apart from any of the political, moral, or legal issues raised by the hijacking incident, it was clear that from a security point of view this airport was in effect a free-fire zone subject to no lawful, responsible authority – a situation that significantly augmented the terrorist threat to all civil aviation in Europe and the Middle East. Secretary Shultz cited figures showing that 15 percent of all international hijackings in the past 15 years had involved

Beirut International Airport.[40] The solution was simple and apparently logical: quarantine the airport. On July 1, the day after the hostages were released, the State Department announced that henceforth no Lebanese airlines would be permitted to fly to the United States and no flights by any airline would be permitted between the United States and Lebanon. An international campaign was launched to secure support for the U.S. position, with Secretary Shultz stating: "We are going to be in touch with our friends about the airport. We hope to develop a concerted plan of action."[41]

The fact that these measures happened to be roughly the same as those called for under the Bonn Declaration in the event of a country's refusal to extradite or prosecute hijackers was significant. Almost immediately after the release of the hostages, the United States had called upon the Lebanese authorities to take the appropriate law enforcement steps toward those responsible for the hijacking and the murder of Robert Stethem. Although the lack of substantive response was due more to Lebanon's basic incapacity to take such steps than to actual refusal on the part of the responsible authorities, Lebanese territory was nonetheless serving as a sanctuary for persons who had committed air piracy and murder. It was thus at least arguable that this was a case for applying the aviation cutoff envisaged in the declaration. Both security and antihijacking policy considerations, therefore, seemed to support the quarantining of Beirut Airport. Unfortunately, however, in presenting this policy the United States apparently devoted insufficient attention to defining and articulating these two operationally congruent but politically, morally, and legally quite distinct sets of considerations. The disappointing international response to the U.S. quarantine campaign may have been partially a result of this failure.

When the Lebanese government protested the U.S. moves and countered with its own campaign to dissuade other countries from joining the sanctions, U.S. arguments that the measures were aimed not against Lebanon per se but against the use of Beirut Airport for terrorism did nothing to mollify Lebanese representatives.[42] The failure to articulate adequately the grounds for the U.S. policy was evident. State Department officials responsible for Near Eastern affairs reportedly were telling the Lebanese ambassador that the measures were not directed against Lebanon, while "senior officials" of the same department were briefing reporters that their objective was to pressure all Lebanese, and thereby the Lebanese government, to prevent terrorism in Beirut.[43] The secretary of state announced on television the evening the TWA hostages were released: "It's not a question of economic sanctions or something like that. It's a question of trying to close the usefulness of that airport."[44] But in an interview the next day he stressed—without, however, explicitly linking it to the airport boycott—the importance of Lebanese cooperation in apprehending those responsible for the incident, calling this a "test" of Lebanon's desire to restore itself to "civilized society."[45] Meanwhile the U.S. announcement of sanctions against Lebanese airlines was officially predicated upon Lebanon's alleged violations of the Hague Convention.[46]

The United States also now began to activate its own law enforcement measures. Even before the hostages' release, Federal Bureau of Investigation agents, empowered by statutes providing worldwide criminal jurisdiction over hijackings of U.S. aircraft and hostage-takings of U.S. citizens, had begun to investigate the hijacking and hostage-taking as a crime under U.S. law.[47] But after the crisis, the U.S. government began to exert such pressure as it could on the Lebanese authorities to apprehend and prosecute or extradite the hijackers.[48] The ubiquitous Nabih Berri, now in his role as justice minister of Lebanon, made it known that he was waiting for action from the public prosecutor before moving to arrest the two original hijackers and that it was "not [his] duty to tell judges how they should proceed." And, straining credulity somewhat, a spokesman claimed that the Amal movement did not even know the identity of the hijackers.[49] Nevertheless, on July 12 Lebanese radio announced that the names of three hijackers had been submitted to the "responsible judicial authorities . . . preparatory to pursuing them and to adopting the appropriate judicial measures against them."[50] The same Amal spokesman who had denied any Amal knowledge of the hijackers' identities the week before now stated that Nabih Berri "does not object to handing the hijackers over for trial."[51]

Meanwhile U.S. allies, summit partners, and others, were showing a distinct lack of enthusiasm toward the airport quarantine campaign. Several of these governments had strongly supported the United States during the crisis itself in condemning the hijacking and seeking diplomatic solutions.[52] They had been most helpful in pursuing action in the relevant international bodies, particularly the ICAO.[53] They had hailed the hostages' release and congratulated the U.S. government on its handling of the crisis.[54] But they did not go along with the key initiative the United States then undertook in response to the perceived causes of the crisis: the airport boycott.

Even while the hostages were still being held, the German government – the Summit Seven host for that year – announced that in late July the Seven's counterterrorism experts' group would meet in Bonn "to discuss steps to combat terrorism in the light of recent acts of terrorism."[55] But as July wore on and not one government, allied or otherwise, joined in the U.S. boycott, it became increasingly evident that the experts' meeting would be highly unlikely to result in any substantive movement toward the U.S. position. Some of the Seven governments, such as the British, Canadian, and Japanese, had appeared more positively inclined toward the U.S. viewpoint than others, such as the French and German; but in the end the airport boycott remained solely a U.S. affair.

Among the reasons cited for this lack of cooperation were Washington's lack of consultation before announcing the sanctions at the beginning of the month, strong Arab diplomatic efforts opposing the sanctions, "special relationships" with Lebanon on the part of the French and also to some extent the Italians, and more fundamental political differences between the United States and West European countries over Middle East policy. Although West European governments (or the airlines themselves) halted flights into Beirut Airport temporarily for security reasons, flights between the airport and Western Europe by Lebanese carriers and others continued, subject in some cases to especially stringent security measures applied by individual countries.[56]

In the face of this universal indifference, the U.S. government began to play down the sanctions aspect of its response to the TWA hijacking, shifting to a lower-key approach that stressed security improvements at the airport. U.S. officials disclaimed any intention of seeking Summit Seven agreement on specific Bonn Declaration sanctions against Lebanon at the late July experts' meeting, though State Department Legal Adviser Abraham D. Sofaer said that should the TWA hijackers not be "brought to justice" the United States "will be faced with the option of seeking action" under the Bonn Declaration. At the same time the Legal Adviser noted: "However persistently we pursue this course, it is a difficult one, depending on the will and courage of seven nations, each with independent interests and views." He also referred to a broader U.S. initiative that had apparently been under way for some time prior to the TWA incident to revitalize the Bonn Declaration by amending it "to provide for a range of sanctions, and for their swift imposition whenever any important aspect of the aviation conventions is violated."[57]

The policies of Western governments taken as a whole in the aftermath of the TWA 847 hijacking revealed some fundamental weaknesses in international counterterrorism cooperation. Despite the successful U.S. handling of the hijacking and hostage crisis itself, with the support of the allies, the Western response following the resolution of the incident was weak and divided. The U.S. government exacerbated the inherent political difficulties of the situation by failing to present coherently and convincingly the mixed motivations—civil aviation security on the one hand, law enforcement and antihijacking policy on the other—underlying its campaign to boycott the airport.

Clearly the actions of the Lebanese government simply did not and could not fit the Bonn Declaration paradigm of a government willfully abetting and harboring hijackers; rather its actions represented feeble efforts to make the best of a situation in which that government was in reality merely one player—and far from the strongest—contending for supremacy in a war-torn, fragmented society. The law enforcement and antihijacking aspect of the U.S. quarantine thus appeared inappropriate and bullying—an image skillfully played upon by Lebanese and Arab diplomacy. The moral wind was thereby taken out of the sails of any possible invocation of the Bonn Declaration against Lebanon. Conversely, the intense political manner in which the United States pursued its international campaign against Beirut Airport, coupled with the campaign's undertone of punitive sanctions against a recalcitrant Lebanon, undermined any effect the United States might have derived from presenting the campaign as motivated by disinterested security concerns.

For their part, several of the other Summit Seven governments failed to consider fully genuine U.S. anger and frustration at a situation in which U.S. carriers and passengers in Europe and the Middle East seemed fair game for any terrorist with a grievance against the United States or Israel. These governments appeared all too willing to pursue a business-as-usual policy toward civil aviation relations with Lebanon in spite of the fact that the situation at Beirut Airport was anything but normal. And they seemed indifferent to the possible repercussions of letting an incident as egregious as the TWA hijacking go by without any sort of coordinated Western response. If the Summit Seven, who with their strongly expressed antihijacking policy represented the leading political forces of the free world as well as the bulk of the world's international aviation traffic, could not formulate a coordinated policy in the wake of an incident of this magnitude, then hopes for the Seven's continued viability as a coordinating mechanism for international counterterrorism cooperation seemed dim indeed.

Despite the failure of the Beirut Airport boycott, in succeeding months the United States vigorously continued its law enforcement efforts aimed at the TWA hijackers. Given the collapsed state of police, prosecutorial, and judicial authorities in Lebanon, where the hijackers were thought to be hiding, however, the chances for bringing any of them to justice seemed remote. But a fortuitous breakthrough occurred in January 1987 when German police arrested two Lebanese men at Frankfurt airport for smuggling explosives. One of the men turned out to be Muhammad Ali Hammadi—identified as one of the two original hijackers of TWA 847. (The other man arrested was Hammadi's brother.) The U.S. government moved quickly to seek his extradition from West Germany for the hijacking and associated crimes, in particular the murder of Robert Stethem.

But the case soon turned into a political quagmire. Two West Germans were abducted in Beirut shortly after Hammadi's arrest, with the kidnappers explicitly linking the hostages' fate to German treatment of Hammadi, in particular his nonextradition to the United States. German and U.S. authorities managed to negotiate around the legal obstacle of the death penalty waiver, but the political obstacle of the German hostages in Beirut proved far less tractable.[58] The German government delayed action on the U.S. extradition request while seeking a solution to its own new Lebanon hostage crisis.[59] A senior German political figure flew to Tehran in late May reportedly to discuss a deal in which the Iranian-influenced kidnappers would release the two Germans in exchange for a quick trial in Germany and light sentences for Hammadi and his brother.

With the Venice summit meeting taking place almost in the midst of this maneuvering, the issue rose to the highest political levels. President Reagan took the position, at least publicly, that extradition per se was less important than ensuring that Hammadi was in fact brought to justice for his crimes, whether in Germany or the United States.[60] U.S. political pressure on Bonn apparently helped quash a deal for Hammadi's release, though it did not succeed in gaining his extradition to the United States.[61] Having allowed a decent interval to elapse since President Reagan's reported personal plea to Chancellor Helmut Kohl at the Venice summit for Hammadi's extradition, the German government announced in late June that the suspect would be tried in Germany for murder and hijacking.[62] German obligations under the Hague Convention were thus fulfilled, and a public dispute between the two governments was avoided, although surely some U.S. officials were privately quite disappointed. The White House issued a statement that although the United States would have preferred extradition of Hammadi, "an expeditious, vigorous, and complete prosecution in Germany of Hamadie with full punishment will satisfy our interest in justice for the victims of Hamadie's crimes while meeting the Federal Republic of Germany's international legal obligations."[63]

The London Libyan People's Bureau Shootings

The incident that thrust the problem of terrorist abuse of diplomatic immunities into the public eye began suddenly on April 17, 1984 in St. James's Square, London, when machine-gun fire from the Libyan mission building in London raked a crowd of anti-Qadhafi demonstrators. A British policewoman on hand to monitor the event was killed, and 10 demonstrators were wounded. British police, legally prohibited from entering the inviolable mission premises, responded by surrounding the building. Shortly thereafter word came from Tripoli that Libyan authorities had likewise surrounded the British embassy there, trapping staff members and the ambassador inside.[64]

Involvement of Libyan diplomatic personnel abroad in acts of violence in their host countries was not a new development. Qadhafi's long-standing campaign against dissident Libyans around the world, often using official Libyan representatives as agents, had included bombings and murder. In fact the immediate backdrop to the shootings in St. James's Square was a series of bombings in London and Manchester just the month before that had injured more than two dozen Arabs. The British police had characterized the bombings as part of the Libyan terror campaign against dissident exiles, and four members of the Libyan diplomatic corps had been expelled for complicity in the incidents.[65] Nor had Britain been the only scene of such incidents. The Libyan embassy in Washington, for example, had been ordered to close by the U.S. government in May 1981 after it had been linked to an attempt to kill a Libyan dissident living in Colorado.[66]

But the shootings in St. James's Square seemed different and somehow more shocking than anything that had gone before. The shots had come directly from within the protected mission premises; the cherished right of free protest had been grossly violated; and above all, the young police constable Yvonne Fletcher had been killed. All seemed to signal a new depth of depravity. Although the murder was not state-directed in the sense that Tripoli had specifically ordered its London representatives to kill a British constable, the violence and sheer recklessness of the shootings, combined with reports that Tripoli had indeed directed its people in London to act aggressively toward the demonstrators, left little doubt where the blame should lie. The British government delivered a sharp protest to Libya, terming the incident an "outrageous abuse of premises" and requesting Libyan government cooperation resolving the matter. But Libya's foreign minister vowed that "we will never allow anyone to go inside our embassy." Tensions between the two countries mounted rapidly.[67]

The precise scope of the applicable legal restrictions on actions by the British authorities was unclear, primarily because of uncertainties about the status of the Libyans inside the mission building in London. The mission had been taken over by revolutionary Libyan students two months before, and its accredited diplomats expelled, without formal notification to the British government. There was thus the possibility that at least some of the occupants of the building would not possess diplomatic immunity from the legal consequences of the shooting. Even if this were the case, however, the building itself was still inviolable; as long as British authorities could not enter the mission to make arrests, whether any particular person inside it had immunity or not was academic. Perhaps even more of a factor in British calculations was the situation of the British embassy and its personnel in Tripoli, as well as the safety of the estimated 8,000 British nationals living and working in Libya. Any direct moves against the Libyan mission in London appeared likely to provoke dangerous retaliation against British interests in Libya itself.[68]

After a few days of futile efforts to secure genuine Libyan cooperation in resolving the situation, the British government broke diplomatic relations with Libya on April 22. The Libyan representatives occupying the mission building in London, as well as all Libyan diplomatic and consular representatives in the United Kingdom, were given one week to leave the country. All British diplomats in Libya were simultaneously recalled. The Foreign Office labeled the April 17 incident "a totally unacceptable and unprecedented breach of British law, international law, and the Vienna Convention on Diplomatic Relations." As for the condition of the several thousand British nationals remaining in Libya, the Foreign Office said: "We have made it clear to the Libyan authorities that we hold them responsible for the safety of our people. . . . We are not at present advising the British community to leave Libya. British residents should consider their position carefully and keep in close touch with developments. . . . "[69]

The Libyan foreign minister's response to the British move was conciliatory, expressing regret but declaring Libya's willingness to "implement the decision peacefully." He played down the threatening noises the government-controlled Libyan press had been making with regard to the British community in Libya.[70] Toward the end of the week, sacks of diplomatic baggage, unsearched by British authorities, began to leave the Libyan mission premises in St. James's Square. It was generally assumed that the murder weapon was in this baggage.[71] The crisis ended, one might say, on schedule as the last British and Libyan representatives left Tripoli and London, respectively, on Sunday, April 29.[72]

From the outset the United States, which had had its own problems with Qadhafi, strongly supported Britain in its confrontation with Libya. France "deplored" Libya's violation of international standards.[73] Some of the United Kingdom's other EC partners were slower in rallying to their beleaguered ally's side. Different countries had varying relationships with Libya. Italy in particular had very close economic ties with Tripoli, dating back to colonial times, and the number of Italians living and working in Libya was much larger than the number of Britons there.[74] Nonetheless, once the immediate crisis was over and the British diplomats were safely returned from Tripoli, the British government pressed ahead with plans for international cooperation in responding to Libya's outrages and initiated consultation with Britain's major allies.

The United States saw the incident as a reminder of the need for Western governments to work together to protect their interests in the face of Libyan supported terrorism. The State Department said: "We hope that other nations will review the record of Libyan activities and that they will arrive at the same conclusions we have regarding the need to demonstrate to Gaddafi meaningful opposition to his policies."[75] West German Chancellor Kohl's visit to London a few days after the end of the crisis occasioned further reassurances of support; the West German foreign minister's previously planned visit to Tripoli was indefinitely postponed.[76] It became evident that the issue would be raised at the London summit meeting the next month; Prime Minister Thatcher made it clear that British policy did not aim at imposing retaliatory economic sanctions upon Libya but more at closer cooperation among Western countries on controlling abuses of diplomatic immunities.[77] At British urging the EC began work on new means to counter state-supported terrorism.[78] British Home Secretary Leon Brittan called for a strengthening of European cooperation in the face of what he described as "the emergence of the terrorist state."[79]

Meanwhile the British government had initiated a reappraisal of the existing rules on diplomatic immunity with a view toward determining if any modification of them could help prevent such incidents in the future. Home Secretary Brittan, in charge of operations during the St. James's Square incident, had expressed his belief early on that the rules of diplomatic immunity codified in the Vienna Convention were inadequate and that Britain should press for changes.[80] A formal Foreign Office review of the "adequacy, operation and enforceability" of the Vienna Convention began immediately upon the conclusion of the crisis; shortly thereafter the House of Commons Foreign Affairs Committee began its own study.[81] The common perception that the law of diplomatic immunity had blocked vigorous British counteraction was somewhat shaken when it came out late in June that the British had had after all the legal right, based on reciprocity with Libya's stated position on the issue, to examine baggage leaving the Libyan mission following the incident, but had refrained for political reasons.[82] Moreover, given the lack of proper accreditation of several of the Libyan representatives involved in the incident, the decision not to detain any of them seemed to be motivated by political rather than legal considerations.

The parliamentary report, which came out in January of the following year, and the government's report, issued three months later, concluded that attempting to amend the Vienna Convention would not be advisable in light of the "difficulties in the way of achieving any restrictive amendment to the Convention, and the doubtful net benefit to the UK of so doing."[83] Rather, the reports concluded, useful measures would include "creation of a climate of opinion that will help prevent abuses of diplomatic immunity and lead to firm action being taken against offending states or individuals," "strict application of the existing provisions of the Vienna Convention," and "introducing restrictive but legally justifiable interpretations of specific provisions of the Vienna Convention where required."[84] British initiatives in international bodies, including the EC and the Summit Seven, were mentioned in the government report as examples of the first category of action; the June 1984 London Summit Declaration and the September 1984 Agreement of the European Community Foreign Ministers on measures to combat terrorism and the abuse of diplomatic immunity were highlighted as results of these initiatives.[85] "New elements of practical and useful cooperation" were noted, including "exchanges of relevant information on diplomats" and "a commitment to common and rigorous practices on matters such as the notification of staff, the size of diplomatic missions and the use of diplomatic premises."[86]

The Berlin Discotheque Bombing

As egregious as Libyan behavior was in the London incident, within two years alleged Libyan terrorist activities abroad would lead to an even more serious confrontation between Qadhafi and a major Western country—this time the United States. Throughout the 1970s, relations between Libya and the United States had been strained at best.[87] But in 1981, the first year of the Reagan administration, they declined even further. In August, U.S. fighters shot down two Libyan jets that had attacked them over international waters in the Gulf of Sidra during U.S. naval maneuvers there; in the fall Libya was implicated in a plot to assassinate the U.S. ambassador in Rome and in an actual attempt on the life of the U.S. chargé d'affaires in Paris; and in November, reports surfaced of Libyan hit squads seeking to enter the United States to assassinate President Reagan.[88]

In the next few years Libya was repeatedly identified by U.S. officials as a key supporter of international terrorism.[89] It was not until the end of 1985, however, that U.S. irritation with Qadhafi's role in terrorist activities around the world crystallized into a decision to act vigorously in opposing his policies. What catalyzed the decision were the coordinated terrorist attacks at the Rome and Vienna airports on December 27, 1985, which killed 20 people (including 5 U.S. citizens) and wounded many others.[90]

Coming almost on the heels of the bloody Egyptair hijacking in November, in which there was strong suspicion of Libyan involvement, the Rome and Vienna attacks galvanized the U.S. government on the subject of Libya and terrorism.[91] U.S. officials concluded that the attacks were perpetrated by the Abu Nidal Palestinian faction and that, as President Reagan put it, "these murderers could not carry out their crimes without the sanctuary and support provided by regimes such as Col. Qadhafi's in Libya. Qadhafi's longstanding involvement in terrorism is well-documented, and there's irrefutable evidence of his role in these attacks."[92] The president charged that "by providing material support to terrorist groups which attack U.S. citizens, Libya has engaged in armed aggression against the United States under established principles of international law, just as if he [sic] had used his own armed forces." In response he announced a range of economic sanctions against Libya, including a prohibition on purchases and imports from and exports to Libya, a ban on U.S.-Libyan maritime and aviation relations, a ban on trade in services relating to projects in Libya, a ban on credits or loans or the transfer of anything of value to Libya or its nationals, a prohibition on transactions relating to travel by Americans to Libya, and the blocking of all official Libyan assets in the United States or in overseas branches of U.S. banks.[93]

The announcement of these unilateral U.S. economic sanctions was accompanied by a strong emphasis on the importance of international cooperation in isolating the Qadhafi regime and a plea to allies not to let business as usual prevent joint action against Libyan-supported terrorism:

> Civilized nations cannot continue to tolerate in the name of material gain and self-interest the murder of innocents. Qadhafi deserves to be treated as a pariah in the world community. We call on our friends in Western Europe and elsewhere to join with us in isolating him. Americans will not understand other nations moving into Libya to take commercial advantage of our departure. We will consult with our key allies to pursue the goal of broader cooperation.[94]

The White House declared that the United States would immediately begin consulting "with allies and other friendly nations in Europe and the Middle East" to secure cooperation for political and economic sanctions against Libya, characterizing such cooperation as "critical." The White House statement ended with a warning that subsequent events would prove to be quite serious: "Should Qadhafi continue his involvement in international terrorism, we're fully prepared to take additional measures."[95] U.S. Deputy Secretary of State John Whitehead was dispatched to West European capitals to attempt to persuade allies to join ranks with the United States.

But the reaction of the major West European states to the U.S. call for support in the anti-Libya campaign was largely negative. Western Europe's economic links with Libya were much more important than those between Libya and the United States, which had been systematically curtailed over the past several years. The United Kingdom, France, West Germany, and Italy all expressed reservations about the wisdom and utility of economic sanctions against Libya.[96] The Whitehead mission met with little success.

The matter was nonetheless placed on the agenda of the regularly scheduled EC foreign ministers meeting in The Hague later in January. Qadhafi, meanwhile, made overtures to the EC, primarily through Italy, aimed at softening the European position toward Libya.[97] At The Hague the ministers expressed strong support for U.S. counterterrorism efforts, but stopped short of joining in economic sanctions against Libya. They did, however, agree not to undercut the U.S. sanctions, pledging to do everything within their power to see that European companies did not seek any commercial advantage from the severance of U.S. economic relations with Libya. They also undertook "not to export arms or other military equipment to countries which are clearly implicated in supporting terrorism," a reference understood to apply to Libya, which was not named directly because of Greek objections.[98]

Tensions between the United States and Libya continued through the spring, heightening drastically in late March when Libyan forces attacked a U.S. naval detachment conducting maneuvers in Libyan-claimed international waters. The U.S. forces sank or damaged three Libyan patrol boats and attacked a missile installation on shore, killing, according to Libyan figures, 56 Libyans.[99] Then on April 5, a bomb destroyed a discotheque in West Berlin packed with U.S. servicemen and others, wounding 204 people and killing a U.S. soldier and a Turkish woman.[100] The U.S. government claimed to have strong evidence that the attack had been directed from Tripoli and referred to a Libyan "master plan" targeting more than 30 U.S. diplomatic facilities and high-ranking diplomats in Europe and the Middle East.[101]

The possibility of a U.S. military strike against Libya in response to the Berlin bombing and other alleged Libyan terrorist plots was openly discussed in Western capitals.[102] U.S. Ambassador to the UN Vernon Walters was sent to West European capitals to obtain support for the U.S. position. An emergency meeting of EC foreign ministers was held on Monday, April 14 at the request of Italy, which, along with Spain and Greece, were the states most opposed to the threatened U.S. action. These Mediterranean countries felt they stood the greatest risk of Libyan retaliation should a U.S. attack take place. Italy, moreover, un-doubtedly hesitated because of its historically close eco-nomic ties with Libya; and Greece, with its rhetorically pro-Arab, anti-American tilt under Prime Minister Andreas Papandreou, had all along been the most hesitant to go along with strong measures. But even West Germany urged Washington to desist from "emotional" action. The Europe-ans feared the terrorist backlash that might result from a U.S. attack, but at the same time did not wish to appear either to be bad allies or too "soft" on terrorism. They reacted to the developing situation by hastily intensifying their own political and economic measures against Libya, while urging restraint on the United States and requesting more detailed evidence of Libya's complicity in terrorism.[103]

The blow fell the night of April 14. Citing Libya's "direct responsibility" for the April 5 Berlin bombing, the White House announced that U.S. military forces had "executed a series of carefully planned air strikes against terrorist-related targets in Libya." The stated targets were "part of Qadhafi's terrorist infrastructure — the command and con-trol systems, intelligence, communications, logistics, and training facilities . . . sites which allow Qadhafi to perpe-trate terrorist acts." The justification for the attack was the U.S. right of self-defense in light of the Berlin bombing and of "clear evidence that Libya is planning future attacks." "It is our hope," the White House statement continued, "that action will preempt and discourage Libyan attacks against innocent civilians in the future."[104] President Reagan said:

> The evidence is now conclusive that the terrorist bomb-ing of LaBelle discotheque was planned and executed under the direct orders of the Libyan regime. On March 25, more than a week before the attack, orders were sent from Tripoli to the Libyan People's Bureau in East Berlin to conduct a terrorist attack against Americans to cause maximum and indiscriminate casualties. Lib-ya's agents then planted the bomb. On April 4, the People's Bureau alerted Tripoli that the attack would

be carried out the following morning. The next day, they reported back to Tripoli on the great success of their mission.[105]

The U.S. representative to the UN submitted a letter formally invoking a U.S. right to self-defense under Article 51 of the UN Charter as the legal basis for the attack, claiming that the United States was responding to "an on-going pattern of attacks by the Government of Libya" that was "in clear violation of Article 2(4) of the United Nations Charter."[106] The different stands taken by West European governments in the period leading up to the U.S. raid on Libya, and the different roles played by the governments in relation to the raid, revealed the sharp divisions between the United States and its European allies on how to deal with state-supported terrorism in general and Libya in particular. Regarding the raid itself, the sharpest contrast among the allies appeared between the United Kingdom, which had given its permission for U.S. planes to operate from bases in Britain to take part in the action, and France, which had refused permission for those same planes to over-fly French territory on their way to and from Libya.

Prime Minister Thatcher had in the period just before the raid seemed reluctant to support U.S. military action, sending public signals that she would oppose the use of British bases to launch operations against Libya.[107] But she went along with the U.S. request, reportedly motivated not only by strong antiterrorist convictions but also by a feeling of political indebtedness for U.S. help in the 1982 Falklands war.[108] The U.S. argument that its action was consistent with Article 51 of the UN Charter was also an important element in the prime minister's approval; she had stated in the past her firm conviction that any action against terrorist-supporting states must be consistent with international legal restrictions on the use of force.[109]

As the lone European ally actively to support the United States, however, the British government drew a storm of domestic criticism, exacerbated by the killing of three British hostages in Lebanon by extremist Arab groups in retaliation for Britain's role in the Libya raid.[110] Prime Minister Thatcher stood firm in the face of this opposition, refusing to rule out further support for U.S. military action against states supporting international terrorism and calling for tougher economic measures against Libya.[111] U.S. officials did their best to help Mrs. Thatcher out of an awkward situation, emphasizing that her permission had been granted only after she had expressed "many questions and concerns."[112] Secretary Shultz referred to British opponents of the bombing in a conciliatory manner, commenting: "I'm always impressed with the common sense of the British people, as I've observed it over a long period of time. . . . When you have [U.S. troops in Europe] attacked, something has to be done about it, and the people, I think, will basically see that point. I certainly hope so."[113]

That senior U.S. figures should give all possible support to an ally who had come through in a critical hour was to be expected. What was more interesting was the manner in which they publicly played down the refusal of France to cooperate, a refusal that had significantly lengthened the distance U.S. planes had to fly to reach Libya, increasing the complications of the mission and the danger to U.S. pilots. Secretary Shultz simply said, "We certainly would have preferred to have that overflight right, but as far as the French view of the matter is concerned, obviously it is for the French to say."[114] He took pains, in fact, to avoid characterizing the French government as soft on terrorism, noting: "France has done some things before and since [the raid] to deal actively with Libyan terrorist threats. . . . They didn't go along with rights to cross their territory, but they are a very active participant in the fight against terrorism."[115]

The secretary could not, however, resist the very diplomatic expression of some exasperation: "As we all recognize, the French are very special to deal with. They are discreet [sic] about each individual thing, and are a joy in some cases and not so much of a joy in others. This is one we didn't enjoy."[116]

The soothing approach taken by U.S. spokesmen toward U.S.-French differences over the affair was extended to the European allies as a whole, all of whom with the exception of Britain had in fact opposed the raid. Secretary Shultz would go no farther than to say of the European governments: "I think in general what we see is a shift in the direction of seeing very clearly what Qadhafi is, what he is doing, and gradually coming more and more to the conclusion that something needs to be done about it. . . . So there is movement. But . . . they do not yet share our conviction that action of this kind is necessary."[117] The secretary attempted to ease fears that divisions revealed by the Libya affair had undermined alliance relationships; and he struck an upbeat, forward-looking tone in his comments on the status and prospects of U.S.-European counterterrorism cooperation:

> So I think that this is one of those cases where, of course, there were differences of view, and we took an action that we felt we had to take. People's views about it varied. On the other hand, the key element here is that we have very quickly coalesced in recognizing the problem and having, really on a much stronger basis than was true, let's say, a week or so ago, a sense of motion and commitment.[118]

In Europe to attend the annual OECD foreign ministers meeting, Deputy Secretary of State Whitehead went out of his way to stress his view that the unity of the alliance had not been harmed: "Disagreements among friends do sometimes occur, but I don't think this is a serious one." He described recent EC steps against Libya as "very positive."[119]

These palliatives masked a real sense of disappointment on the part of U.S. officials at the attitudes of most European allies, which came through in some public statements.

As Secretary Shultz put it, "We were able to mount this operation entirely over water with no help from any of the continental European countries, and it's too bad we had to do it that way but we did it."[120] Defense Secretary Caspar Weinberger was blunter, expressing "considerable disappointment" with the French government (though not mentioning Spain, which had similarly refused overflight permission).[121] In this light President Reagan's statement in his speech announcing the raid the night of April 14 may have carried a more pointed meaning than appeared on the surface: "To our friends and allies who cooperated in today's mission, I would only say you have the permanent gratitude of the American people. Europeans who remember history understand better than most that there is no security, no safety in the appeasement of evil."[122]

Despite such feelings, evidently the U.S. government had decided to treat publicly the unconcealable divisions between the United States and its European allies over the Libya raid as passing tactical differences that would not adversely affect future counterterrorism cooperation or relations in general. For their part, European governments moved quickly in the aftermath of the raid to stake out tougher positions on Libya, demonstrating their rectitude both to Washington and to those segments of their own electorates that wanted a firmer stance on terrorism. They quite naturally had their own anxieties about a split between Europe and the United States over this emotionally charged affair. The EC foreign ministers met in a second emergency session three days after the raid. British Foreign Secretary Geoffrey Howe, as well as the foreign ministers of West Germany and Italy, warned of possible damage to the alliance and agreed that Qadhafi "must not be allowed to succeed where Moscow has failed" in splitting the West. But stronger EC action against Libya continued to be obstructed by Greece.[123]

The third meeting in two weeks of EC foreign ministers to discuss the Libya situation was held April 23. Rejecting the recommendation of an EC monitoring group report that all Libyan People's Bureaus in Western Europe should be closed (an option strongly favored by Britain, which had had no diplomatic relations with Libya since April 1984), the ministers did decide upon a drastic reduction in the number of Libyan diplomats in their countries and stricter surveillance of those remaining as well as of nonofficial Libyans such as students. They also called for an end to the subsidized sale of food to Libya; for the time being the European commission ended only the sale of subsidized butter, taking other subsidized food sales under review.[124]

European governments responded immediately to the EC decisions. West Germany ordered the Libyan staff in Bonn reduced from 41 to 19. France announced its intention to apply the measures agreed to by the EC.[125] The British expelled 21 nonofficial Libyans for "organizing student revolutionary activity."[126] The U.S. government applauded the EC moves, with UN representative Walters declaring: "The United States welcomes these actions as part of the response which free societies need to protect themselves."[127] The day after the EC foreign ministers session, senior U.S. and West European law enforcement officials met in The Hague for talks on closer cooperation against Libyan and other international terrorism. British Home Secretary Douglas Hurd commented that the West's counterterrorism machinery had "moved decisively into higher gear."[128]

Despite the new impetus that seemed to have been given to joint counterterrorism efforts, the discord between the United States and Western Europe over the Libya raid was real. Commentators used phrases like "more mutual bad temper across the Atlantic than perhaps anything since the Second World War."[129] The greater vulnerability of European countries to retaliation, given their relative proximity to terrorist sources, was a key reason for the widespread opposition to U.S. military action. Italian Prime Minister Bettino Craxi worried that the U.S. action was likely to unleash "explosions of fanaticism and of criminal and suicide missions."[130] Western Europe further feared that Libya might

be pushed into the arms of the Soviets, with grave consequences for the balance of power in the Mediterranean.[131]

In Britain, these concerns were augmented by a certain
degree of public resentment over the government's role in
the raid and the increased vulnerability of British nationals
to terrorist retaliation, already graphically demonstrated
by the fate of the three British hostages in Lebanon. More
than half of the Britons surveyed in an opinion poll believed
their government had been too supportive of U.S. policy
toward Libya; two-thirds believed the U.S. raid was wrong;
and over 80 percent believed it would increase the likelihood
of terrorist attacks on Britain.[132] An even greater margin of
West Germans — three-quarters of the sample — disapproved
of the raid. But in France, whose government had been the
most conspicuous dissenter, public feelings were much more
positive: almost two-thirds approved of the U.S. action, and
40 percent felt their government had not supported U.S.
policy toward Libya enough. In the United States itself,
meanwhile, a strong 70 percent of the public approved of
the raid, and feelings of resentment against European —
particularly French — lack of cooperation ran high.[133]

Perhaps alarmed by the depth of disagreement revealed
in these polls, as well as by the widely divergent positions
taken by key governments, Western leaders tried in the following weeks to reduce political acrimony and establish a
more harmonious position on Libya. At the British-French
meeting in London on April 27, for example, Prime Minister Jacques Chirac tried to smooth over the contradictory
positions of the two countries on the raid: "I think [Mrs.
Thatcher] understood that we do not have the same point of
view and took a different position from the British," he said,
"but that doesn't make any problems between Britain and
France."[134]

The U.S. government focused on forging a common position against terrorism in general and Libya in particular
to be adopted jointly at the forthcoming Tokyo summit.
Given the evident widespread European unhappiness with
the Libya raid, the challenge was to persuade the West Eu-

ropeans that it had been an unfortunate necessity, resorted to reluctantly by a U.S. government left with no alternative in the face of Libyan ferocity and the passivity of major allies, rather than the emotional response of a trigger-happy administration obsessed with Qadhafi and thirsting for an excuse to strike at him. The corollary of the first view, of course, was that stronger nonmilitary measures on the part of the Western democracies acting together could both help prevent terrorism and forestall further need for violent U.S. responses to it; the corollary of the second view was that the United States was a dangerous partner in the fight against terrorism and that the Europeans would be better off not tying their fortunes too closely to those of the Americans in this area. U.S. explanations of the raid in international forums therefore claimed that the United States had tried everything else first before being forced into taking military action. As Ambassador Walters had put it in the UN the day after the attack:

> The United States took these measures of self-defense only after other repeated and protracted efforts to deter Libya from its ongoing attacks against the United States in violation of the Charter. But when quiet diplomacy, public condemnation, economic sanctions, and demonstrations of military force failed to dissuade Col. Qadhafi, this self-defense action became necessary.[135]

There was evidence from European capitals that the message was getting through. Foreign Secretary Howe commented: "There obviously was a connection between the slowness with which the EEC was reacting to terrorism and the view of the US."[136] Chancellor Kohl admitted that "too frequently, the Europeans have been too satisfied with mere declarations which have been politically ineffectual while leaving the U.S. alone in its struggle against international terrorism. . . . If we Europeans do not want to follow the Americans for reasons of our own, we must develop political initiatives."[137] President Mitterrand rather suddenly adopted a strong antiterrorist stance, calling for an international antiterrorist organization and asserting that "France is one of the rare countries which fight effectively against terrorism." He explained the French refusal to allow a U.S. overflight by saying: "We do not wish, under the guise of the fight against terrorism, that France be involved in international action which it has not freely examined."[138]

As to specific measures, U.S. officials had not entirely given up the idea of inducing the Europeans to join in the campaign to isolate Libya economically. But the bombs that had fallen on Tripoli were not powerful enough to shake the deep-rooted European skepticism about the effectiveness of economic sanctions in principle, nor to weaken West European–Libyan economic ties.[139] Even the United Kingdom showed itself hesitant to support such measures. Foreign Secretary Howe commented in Parliament on April 23: "The point about economic sanctions has been frequently dealt with. Experience of cases when it has been used previously demonstrate that it has not proved an effective weapon."[140]

Political and diplomatic measures were, however, another matter. EC actions in the week following the raid had demonstrated that the earlier European resistance to singling out Libya as a source of terrorism and taking strict measures against the Libyan official and nonofficial presence in Western Europe had been largely overcome. U.S. officials, encouraged by this trend, looked for success at the summit. Speaking of his expectations for the Tokyo meeting, Secretary Shultz said: "The Europeans can see it as clearly as we do. After all, most of these terrorist acts are taking place in Europe, so I'm sure there is going to be a very strong unanimity of view on the importance of having a strategy and a tactical ability to implement it."[141]

The declaration that emerged from the Tokyo summit, as described earlier, was as strongly worded as could have been hoped. Most important for purposes of the current discussion, Libya was singled out explicitly as a state supporter of terrorism, giving at least the public impression of

unanimity among the allies on the issue — a significant political success that did much to dispel the picture of discord
created by the events surrounding the U.S. raid itself.

In the aftermath of Tokyo, U.S. officials were more open
about the political link they perceived between the Libya
raid and the change in European attitudes that had led to
stronger EC actions in late April and the tough Tokyo summit declaration. They also traced the already evident substantial decrease in Middle Eastern–linked terrorism in Europe to the bombing. Director of the State Department
Office for Counter-Terrorism Robert Oakley analyzed the
raid's effects in early June:

> What· has been the result of this limited act of self-
> defense? First, a marked reduction in Qadhafi-support-
> ed terrorism, apparently due to internal Libyan disar-
> ray, the compromise of Libya's external terror network,
> and the tighter controls placed upon Libyan activities
> all around the world by governments more determined
> than before to avoid terrorism in their countries. Sec-
> ond, a sudden awakening of European and other gov-
> ernments to the serious dangers posed by international
> terrorism and a new willingness to work together to
> deter and prevent it.[142]

On June 30 the United States intensified economic
sanctions against the Qadhafi regime still further, prohibit-
ing all operations by U.S. companies in Libya, tightening
restrictions on exports of U.S. components and parts that
might be destined for Libya, and, "in consultation with our
European allies," pursuing a ban on imports into the United
States of petroleum products refined in third countries from
Libyan crude oil. The stated purpose of the new measures
was "to demonstrate that [the United States Government]
will not entertain even the appearance of continuing to do
business as usual with Qadhafi."[143]

What have been the effects of these measures? The U.S.
economic sanctions and the limited cooperation given to
them by the Europeans, combined with the overall drop in

world oil prices, have definitely affected the Libyan economy.[144] Whether this has in turn affected Libyan willingness
to support acts of terrorism abroad is impossible to say. The
direct longer-term military results of the April 1986 raid
appear to have been limited, but the psychological-political
dislocation may have been considerably greater—in any
event, since the raid there has been an undeniable lessening
of Libyan-supported terrorist activity abroad.[145] And even
more important in the long run, by the restrained and
thoughtful manner in which both the United States and its
European allies handled the aftermath of the raid, the hard
feelings of the night of April 14 among the allies were
turned into a strong cooperative stance in Tokyo only three
weeks later, demonstrating restored and enhanced solidarity on the issue of terrorism and fostering a distinct im-
provement in the political environment for collective counterterrorism efforts.

The El Al Bombing Attempt

On April 17, 1986 El Al security at Heathrow airport dis-
covered a bomb in the luggage of an Irish woman about to
board a jumbo jet bound for Tel Aviv. The woman had been
duped into carrying the bomb by her Jordanian boy-
friend, Nizar Hindawi, by whom she was five months preg-
nant at the time. Hindawi was quickly arrested by British
authorities.[146]

Questions of possible Syrian government involvement
in the plot arose quickly. The Israeli government charged in
early May that the bombing attempt was "planned and carried out by part of the established organization of the security and intelligence community of Syria." Three weeks after
Hindawi's arrest, the British government requested a waiver of diplomatic immunity for three attachés at the Syrian
embassy in London in order to question them about the
bomb attempt. When the request was refused, the three
were expelled from the country. A fourth Syrian diplomat,

reportedly in charge of Syrian military intelligence operations in Britain, left the country the next day. Three British diplomats were expelled from Syria in retaliation for the British action.[147]

The notion that the Syrian government might be behind acts of international terrorism was hardly a new one. The U.S. government, for example, had carried Syria on a list of countries providing "repeated support for acts of international terrorism" since 1979; as a 1986 State Department paper put it, "Syria clearly has a long record of involvement in terrorism." Apart from direct Syrian official support for acts of terror, a number of quasi-independent terrorist groups whose activities were "generally in line with Syrian objectives" were provided bases and training facilities in Syria and Syrian-occupied areas of Lebanon. The most notorious of these was the Abu Nidal organization, called the "most active and brutal international terrorist group operating today." Abu Nidal operatives were, according to the State Department report, provided with travel documents and logistical support by the Syrian government and permitted to operate facilities in Damascus. Several other radical Palestinian organizations, as well as other non–Middle Eastern terrorist groups, were also receiving Syrian support. The report listed almost 50 acts of international terrorism going back to 1983 in which Syrian agents or terrorist groups operating out of Syria or Syrian-controlled territory were implicated.[148]

Despite this record, however, Western leaders were cautious in their comments about the Syrian role in the El Al bomb plot while the prosecution of Hindawi went forward through the summer and fall. The U.S. government was rather equivocal; Secretary of State Shultz acknowledged the evidence against Syria, saying that "we have no reason to doubt" the Israeli allegations of Syrian involvement. The White House noted, however, that it would be "premature" to draw conclusions until the British investigation was completed. Two other important themes surfaced in U.S. commentary: Syria's constructive role in negotiating for the

release of Western hostages in Lebanon and the progress
Syria was making in shutting down the terrorist and terror-
ist-front groups headquartered in Damascus.[149] Syria's central role in Middle East politics makes it indispensable to
any meaningful regional peace process—more reason for
Western governments to tread softly on the subject of official Syrian involvement in this terrorist attempt.

With the opening of the Hindawi trial in October, however, it became painfully clear that the problem of Syrian
government support for the El Al bombing attempt would
have to be confronted. The prosecution unequivocally
charged that the Syrian government had not just aided, but
had planned and directed, the bomb plot and that Hindawi
had been helped in London by a Syrian embassy official and
had contacted the Syrian ambassador after the attempt
had failed.[150]

The storm burst with Hindawi's conviction on October
24. With the trial over, the full implications of the existing
evidence, judicial and extra-judicial, of Syrian backing for
the bomb attempt had to be faced. Foreign Secretary
Geoffrey Howe, announcing that "there is conclusive
evidence of Syrian official involvement with Hindawi,"
summed up the record to the House of Commons: Hindawi
had entered Britain on an official Syrian passport under
a false name; the Syrian ambassador had been person-
ally involved in communications between Hindawi and
Syrian intelligence services several months before the
attempt; Hindawi had met with the Syrian ambassador in
the embassy after the discovery of the bomb; he had spent
the night after the bombing attempt in a Syrian embassy
safe house; and during his detention he had attempted to
contact Syrian intelligence officials in Damascus to seek
their help in securing his release. Declaring the involvement of "the ambassador, members of his staff, and the
Syrian authorities in Damascus" with Hindawi's crime
"unacceptable," the foreign secretary announced the immediate severing of diplomatic relations between the United
Kingdom and Syria and the tightening of security controls

on incoming Syrian flights. He also stated that the government was "taking urgent steps to inform our European partners, and other friendly governments, about the details of the case and the measures we are taking" and would be "impressing on them the wider security implications of the involvement of the Syrian authorities and urging them to take appropriate supporting action." The government's moves were strongly supported by all political parties.[151]

The Syrian ambassador in London denied all charges of involvement in the bomb attempt, calling it a joint U.S. and Israeli intelligence plot.[152] Syrian President Hafiz al-Assad reacted angrily to the British cutoff of diplomatic ties, ordering British diplomats to leave Damascus in one week (half the time given Syrian diplomats to depart London) and closing Syrian airspace and harbors to British aircraft and ships. The Syrian government did, however, officially promise to protect the lives and property of the 250 Britons living in the country.[153]

The United States immediately withdrew its own ambassador from Damascus in support of the British stand. The White House announced intentions to take further actions against Syria: "A state that encourages and takes part in terrorism isolates itself from the civilized world. The United States will consult and cooperate with others to bring practical meaning to the isolation."[154] Other major allies took no quick steps regarding Syria. The French simply said the matter would be discussed among EC members. The West Germans, handling their own trial of a Hindawi (Ahmad Hasi, Nizar's brother) on charges of participation in the March 29, 1986 bombing of the German-Arab Friendship Union in Berlin, had no immediate comment.[155]

The chances for a vigorous, united European reaction against Syria appeared to suffer a serious blow when it became known the day after the Hindawi verdict that France was on the verge of concluding a new $300 million contract to sell arms to Syria. Aside from economic concerns, moreover, another consideration seemed to lie behind French reluctance to take a strong stand: the fate of the 8

French hostages held by Syrian-backed groups in Lebanon. London's expectations of EC support were not high for the measures it planned to request of its partners: a curb on high-level exchanges, decreases in Syrian embassy staffs in European countries and tighter surveillance of those remaining, recall of EC ambassadors from Damascus, heightened security measures to be applied to Syrian flights, and suspension of arms sales.[156] And indeed, the October 27 meeting of EC foreign ministers declined to support the British request for these joint measures. The participants would go no further than to sign a statement expressing "a common sense of outrage" at the alleged Syrian involvement in the bomb plot (Greece refused even to sign the statement). Foreign Secretary Howe said that the Twelve were sending "a less adequate signal to Syria than we would have wished" and announced that Britain would block further EC aid to Damascus. Some EC officials, however, complained privately that Britain had not fully consulted its partners before breaking off relations with Syria. All political parties in the United Kingdom reacted with disappointment and anger to the EC's failure to support London.[157]

In the ensuing couple of weeks, however, European support for a tougher stance began to coalesce. In early November France announced that it would accept a modified British package of proposals for action against Syria, including a halt in arms sales, suspension of visits to EC countries by ranking Syrian officials, and closer surveillance of Syrian diplomatic buildings and of Syrian flights.[158] On November 10 the EC foreign ministers agreed to the adoption of these proposals.[159]

Four days later Washington announced its own series of measures against Syria. Noting that the Hindawi conviction had "directly implicated the Syrian Government in the attempted bombing of the El Al airplane," the White House stated:

> We believe further steps must be taken to discourage such Syrian behavior and to express our outrage, and

that of the American people, at Syrian sponsorship of this attack and its long pattern of support for terrorism. We have been in consultation with our allies on this matter, including members of the European Economic Community who announced their own measures on November 10. We welcome these decisions. These measures and our own actions will send a clear and unequivocal message to Syria: Its support of terrorism is unacceptable to the international community of nations.

Adding to sanctions already in place, including special treatment of militarily significant exports to Syria and a foreign aid cutoff, the White House announced a further tightening of export controls on national security items, termination of export-import programs for Syria, termination of the air transport agreement between the United States and Syria, a ban on the sale of Syrian Arab Airlines tickets in the United States, a reduction of U.S. embassy staff in Damascus, and a suspension of high-level Syrian visits to the United States. The White House announcement concluded:

These measures are intended to convince the Syrian Government that state support of terrorism will not be tolerated by the civilized world. . . . Syria can play an important role in a key part of the world but it cannot expect to be accepted as a responsible power or treated as one as long as it continues to use terrorism as an instrument of its foreign policy.[160]

Reinforcing the joint stance of the major democracies, Japan announced on November 11 that it would also implement the measures adopted by the EC foreign ministers against Syria.[161]

Once the EC and U.S. sanctions had been instituted, the British government soft-pedaled its earlier expressions of disappointment at the lukewarm support of its European partners. In Paris for a bilateral summit later in November, for example, Prime Minister Thatcher avoided journalists' questions about her disappointment with the French attitude on Syria by stressing the "great support" the EC had given her.[162]

A number of inescapable and delicate considerations were hanging over allied policy toward Syria in response to its publicly demonstrated involvement in such a heinous act, as well as its whole record of official support for numerous terrorist attacks over several years. One was the question of Syria's role in Middle East politics. Unlike Libya, Syria is a central player in Middle East peace efforts; and unlike Colonel Qadhafi, President Assad is an influential leader in the region and the Arab world, not to be brushed aside lightly.

Even the tone of Western statements announcing sanctions against Syria was quite different from that with regard to Libya. If Libya had been treated contemptuously, as an outcast, Syria seemed to be treated more like a difficult child that would now have to be punished, but whose place in the family of nations was being held open for readmission as soon as its behavior improved. As a British diplomatic source put it: "There are many reports that Syria, Libya, and Iran are involved in a network of terrorism but in diplomatic terms there is a different weight attached to Syria. It is the cornerstone of the Middle East."[163]

East-West rivalry was of course a factor as well. Syrian-Soviet links were quite strong; there was a substantial Soviet presence in Syria, and Moscow had given Damascus political backing in its confrontation with the Western countries following the Hindawi trial.[164] Yet another factor complicated the Western approach. Syria's highly sophisticated intelligence networks and links to the most dangerous international terrorist groups such as Abu Nidal gave it a capacity to retaliate against Western interests that was considerably greater than that of the relatively amateurish Libyans. And finally, there was the matter of Syrian influence over the groups holding Western hostages in Lebanon; Damascus's key role in the release of the 1985 TWA hostages was not forgotten. In fact, just the day after approving the EC sanctions against Syria, the French government publicly thanked Damascus for its role in the freeing of two French hostages who had been held in Lebanon.[165]

All in all, it seemed more sensible for the West to fashion a limited response to Syrian support for terrorism, linking the response to specific acts, most notably, of course, the El Al bomb plot, and ameliorating it as soon as the Syrian attitude improved, rather than waging a campaign to isolate the country as it had with Libya. It suffices to note that (leaving aside the very different calculations necessary in case of military action) Syria, unlike Libya, has not even been named as a supporter of terrorism by the Summit Seven—this despite its even more clearly demonstrated connection to an act of terrorism that, had it succeeded, would have been far more devastating than the April 1986 Berlin discotheque bombing for which such severe punishment had been meted out to Libya. And indeed, as soon as a decent interval had passed without the occurrence of further blatant Syrian-supported terrorism and certain signs of an improved attitude had appeared, notably the closure of some terrorists' offices in Damascus, Western countries began to relax their stand. On July 13, 1987 EC foreign ministers (with the exception of the British) agreed to lift the ban on high-level contacts imposed in November 1986. The announcement was made to the accompaniment of hopeful statements about the Middle East peace process. Most of the other sanctions imposed in November were left in place for the time being.[166] And on September 2 the United States, citing the closure of Abu Nidal's Damascus office and improved Syrian behavior in the Middle East, returned its ambassador to Damascus.[167]

4

Essentials of a Collective Response

Clearly the United States and its major allies do not formulate their responses to state-supported terrorism in a political vacuum. Western counterterrorism cooperation is but one link in the complex web of relationships among the industrialized democracies. To place the subject in full context is a task well beyond the scope of this study, but certain features emerge so prominently from the case studies presented above that they must be briefly addressed here. These relate to the differing perspectives that the United States, on the one hand, and its major European allies, on the other, bring to this problem.

First, the U.S. experience with international terrorism is unique. Although the United States is the most prominent terrorist target internationally, it has so far been almost entirely spared the sort of terrorist violence at home that all the major European democracies have had to confront. For the Europeans, state-supported international terrorism has been a problem of domestic security as well as foreign policy. This aspect of the threat inevitably places the question of a collective response in a rather different light. It is serious enough when your citizens traveling or working abroad are exposed to the danger of a bombing, a hostage-taking, or a hijacking. When the bombs are going off or the hostages are being seized in your own cities, however, the political repercussions are of a different order of magnitude. It is not surprising that governments faced with such a threat may approach high-profile international statements and actions somewhat more cautiously.

Second, Western Europe's relationship to the Middle East is quite different from the United States, for various reasons: geographic proximity; economic (especially energy) links; historical, social, and cultural ties; and a somewhat greater reluctance to support Israel against its Arab adversaries. Such factors make European countries more hesitant than the United States to participate in vigorous measures against Middle Eastern countries accused of supporting terrorism. The United Kingdom is somewhat of an exception, but an exception that to some extent proves the rule: Its greater distance from the centers of violence and its energy self-sufficiency help Britain overcome the kinds of reservations continental governments have shown about taking firm action. In general, the Europeans seem considerably more sensitive than the United States to the broader foreign policy repercussions of counterterrorism policies.

Another layer of complexity is added by the institutional framework within which Western collective counterterrorism efforts take place. The Summit Seven suffers from some notable drawbacks as a vehicle for such efforts. Because it is an annual meeting of heads of state, it is inherently unwieldy and slow to act. Terrorism is at most only one of several important issues facing the participants, as at Bonn in 1978 or Tokyo in 1986; and more often it is simply a peripheral matter to be addressed once more pressing economic and political issues are out of the way, or not at all, as at most of the other summits. The Seven includes neither the smaller industrialized democracies nor a range of other potentially sympathetic countries that could contribute to a successful collective effort. The group possesses no permanent staff to monitor either events that might trigger sanctions or the effects of any sanctions imposed. And it possesses practically no real guidelines, other than the terse and often vague language of the summit declarations themselves, for determining when and how to impose or terminate any measures. The very mandate of the Seven to address terrorism at all is constantly questioned by some of its members, notably France—though it is precisely the Seven's lack of any formal structural guidelines that makes one wonder what the basis of such legalistic objections could be.

It would be wrong, however, to paint too bleak a picture of the Summit Seven as a vehicle for counterterrorism, because it also has a number of unique advantages. The level of the participants (heads of state and government) may make it harder to get their attention, but can ensure maximum political weight for any pronouncements on an issue, once attention is obtained. Similarly, the wide scope of issues addressed by the participants can cause a single topic to be lost in the shuffle, but can also facilitate a more comprehensive approach than could a forum with a narrower focus. The group's exclusivity may make it harder to incorporate other states in its efforts, but can also make it easier to secure consensus and adopt decisions. The lack of formal structures and guidelines that can impede collective measures can also liberate the group from the technical-legal constraints more formally established entities must confront. These potential advantages have so far been only feebly exploited, less because of structural flaws than because of differing attitudes toward collective action against terrorism and the proper role of the Seven.

To be sure, a sort of creeping institutionalization of Summit Seven activities has occurred, not only in terrorism but in several other economic and political areas. Students of summitry have noted that national attitudes on this matter differ, with the United States tending to encourage greater formality and operational detail and with Europeans resisting these trends.[1] To expand the Seven's counterterrorism efforts effectively would be difficult without more structured procedures to address the inevitable operational questions, but this need not and probably will not lead to the actual formation of an international staff or secretariat. Rather, less formal parallel procedures could be created where necessary within each government to ensure more effective and consistent attention to collective efforts.

The activities of the EC are also particularly relevant to this discussion. The EC has witnessed extensive counterterrorism work on several levels—security, intelligence, and law enforcement as well as collective political action. In the latter area, EC initiatives have, given the overlap in membership, at times intersected with Summit Seven efforts. In the spring of 1986, for example, the EC was a forum for the European states to work out positions and adopt measures on Libyan-supported terrorism in response to U.S. initiatives that led to steps by the Summit Seven. On other occasions, as when dealing with Syria in the fall of 1986, the EC has been the primary channel of cooperative measures, with the United States taking supportive action.

Some European countries—France particularly, but not exclusively—appear to feel more comfortable with the EC than with the Summit Seven as a channel for collective political measures. Some of the major French objections to a more vigorous Seven posture—the question of "mandate" and the dangers of creating a "world directorate" and fostering North-South divisions—would seem, however, to apply to EC activities as well. The real advantage of the EC as a counterterrorism channel from this point of view, of course, is that it does not include the United States. The attractions are twofold: the relative political weight of the major European states is greater within the EC than within the Seven, and their counterterrorism measures in the EC context are relatively free of the sometimes uncomfortable association with U.S. policies in the Middle East or elsewhere over which they have no control. But even from a less political perspective the EC does offer some advantages in counterterrorism work not matched by the Summit Seven, particularly its far more developed legal and institutional structures for adopting, monitoring, and terminating political or economic sanctions.

The Summit Seven and the EC are, however, not naturally competitive or mutually exclusive in counterterrorism efforts. Indeed, Summit Seven work in general has consistently included EC representatives, setting a pattern for communication and cooperation in such areas as counterterrorism. Gatherings that bridge the membership of the two bodies, such as the May 1987 Paris meeting of cabinet-level Summit Seven and EC officials responsible for counterterrorism, are a positive (though still tentative) sign, as is the intensified liaison between senior U.S. and EC counterterrorism officials since 1986. Such direct links, however, have so far taken place in a security–law enforcement context, rather than a diplomatic-political one. Although they do help engender a more positive overall atmosphere in Western counterterrorism cooperation, extending the precedent directly into the political area will be considerably trickier. Parallel actions supported by intensive ad hoc consultation may prove more feasible for the time being.

Despite these built-in differences and complexities, this examination of the cases in which collective action against state-supported terrorism has been attempted reveals certain common elements that can markedly affect such action. These elements are categorized here by four main themes: consensus, credibility, clarity, and consistency.

Consensus

The key role of consensus in collective action is perhaps best highlighted by the Western response to the revelations of Syrian backing for the April 1986 London El Al bomb attempt that emerged at the trial of Nizar Hindawi in October of that year. Initially the EC governments reacted negatively to joint measures requested by Britain almost immediately after the trial. But the British persisted, and within a matter of days European support for a tougher stand began to coalesce. Only two weeks after they had declined to support the British request for joint measures against

Syria, EC foreign ministers agreed to a modified package of British proposals comprising most of the measures they had initially rejected. The appearance of Western disunity and weakness was replaced by a show of solidarity and firmness. U.S. measures of support included immediate withdrawal of the U.S. ambassador from Damascus and a substantial tightening of existing economic and national security measures against Syria, as well as other diplomatic sanctions paralleling those of the EC. That show of solidarity has now, in the view of EC governments as well as the United States, helped to elicit the desired response from Damascus.

The contrast with other cases where such cohesiveness was not present—such as the Western response in the aftermath of the TWA 847 hijacking—is striking and further underlines the importance of consensus. These cases illustrate that it is important, before deciding on a course of action, to ask this question: Will severe measures imposed by one or two governments without the support of allies have a greater overall effect than a set of somewhat less severe, but still effective, measures imposed on a truly collective basis? Admittedly the latter is not always easy or even possible to achieve. A convincing show of unity, however, does not necessarily require that all involved governments adopt exactly the same measures, but simply that the measures they adopt are in the aggregate serious enough to demonstrate unity of purpose.

Credibility

The effective maintenance of norms—that is, the rule of law—in any society is undermined to the extent that violations of those norms are seen as unpunished, or to the extent that they are selectively punished based on extraneous factors. This applies as well at the international level. Every failure to respond strongly to an instance of state-supported terrorism undermines the norms against it and reveals the apparent weakness of those states that have an interest in upholding such norms. Conversely, an effective demonstration of determination to oppose terrorism strengthens the reputation of such states and helps foster an atmosphere in which the prohibitions against state-supported terrorism are taken more seriously.

The Summit Seven response to the hijacking of an Air India plane to South Africa by armed mercenaries in late 1981 illustrates this point. When the South African government released the hijackers without charges, Britain and the United States warned that failure to take proper law enforcement measures against them would probably result in an aviation cutoff. The South African stance quickly reversed, and the hijackers were soon tried, convicted, and sentenced to prison terms. What is noteworthy about this case is its timing. Occurring just after the announcement of aviation sanctions against Afghanistan, Summit Seven pressure on a country to deal strictly with hijackers carried weight. Unfortunately, the potential benefits of this strong, credible Western stance displayed in South Africa were dissipated by subsequent years of inaction during numerous hijacking incidents. It will not be easy for the Summit Seven and like-minded countries to reestablish the reputation they had in 1981.

On the other hand, although direct causal links are impossible to prove, it is at least arguable that the strength shown by the West in its response in 1986 to Libyan involvement in terrorism has played some role in the marked subsequent decrease in Libyan-supported international terrorism, as well as international terrorism in general. How permanent this decrease will prove is, of course, open to question, but it does seem reasonable to assume that the combined effect of the U.S. military action followed closely by strong demonstrations of united Western political opposition to Libyan-supported terrorism has been significant, not only for its immediate target but also for a wider audience.

Clarity

The attempt to achieve collective enforcement of international counterterrorism norms can fall apart when confronted with the complex and ambiguous realities of specific situations. The Western response in the aftermath of the hijacking of TWA Flight 847 to Beirut in 1985 is an excellent example. The U.S. call for a boycott of Beirut International Airport was based on a confusing mixture of rationales: on the one hand, it was presented as a measure dictated by politically neutral considerations of civil aviation security, and on the other, as a step designed to pressure the Lebanese government to restore normalcy at the airport and to take law enforcement measures against those responsible for the hijacking.

The latter rationale, however strongly it may have reflected understandable U.S. frustration and anger over the hijacking and the untenable conditions at Beirut Airport, simply did not appear justified by the situation in Lebanon. How could the government of Lebanon be held responsible for security at the airport when that government represented merely one — and far from the strongest — force contending for supremacy in a war-torn, fragmented society? How could the normal procedures of apprehension and prosecution of the perpetrators be undertaken when the government authorities formally responsible for such steps did not even have the capacity to conduct a routine criminal trial — when, in fact, the minister of justice himself, Nabih Berri, had arguably been an accomplice to the hostage-taking that followed the hijacking?

The initial rationale — that of simply avoiding a dangerous airport — would not, on the other hand, seem to justify the campaign Washington was waging for an international boycott. After all, when the State Department issues a travel advisory, it does not normally launch an international campaign to induce foreign governments to follow suit. Certainly other governments whose airlines had been flying into Beirut were capable of judging the security risks independently and acting accordingly. Indeed, West European airlines, acting on their own or at the behest of their governments, did suspend flights into Beirut Airport for security considerations, although flights between Beirut and Western Europe by Lebanese and other carriers continued. Further, the unmistakable undertone of punitive sanctions in the quarantine campaign made Washington's arguments based purely on aviation security appear somewhat disingenuous.

Not surprisingly, the international response to the U.S. campaign was nil. Even the most skillfully presented justifications might not, of course, have elicited widespread support for the U.S. initiative, given all the other political and economic obstacles to it; the presence of such obstacles, however, merely underlines the importance of carefully selecting and clearly presenting the rationale for a policy of collective response to terrorism in such complex situations.

In contrast, the British and allied response to the London Libyan People's Bureau incident was firm but measured and (after some understandable initial confusion) based on a relatively clear perception of the relevant legal principles and political realities. The system of diplomatic protection, though subject to possible abuse, was still basically a healthy and necessary part of international life; such abuses could be adequately handled within the system, and radical changes were neither necessary nor desirable. The incident itself was resolved satisfactorily; rather than undermining the structure of diplomatic immunities, it strengthened the Western governments' understanding of, and willingness to employ, the protective powers inherent in that structure against governments that would exploit it for terrorist purposes.

Consistency

The most difficult and most important element of collective counterterrorism action is finding the proper balance between the preservation of principle and the exigencies of

politics and economics. The aviation cutoff imposed by the
Summit Seven against Afghanistan in 1981 for that country's failure to extradite or prosecute the hijackers of a Pakistani jet is revealing in this respect. What answer could the
Summit Seven give to the Afghan complaint that many
other countries had harbored hijackers without being
subjected to sanctions? When the democracies impose
ostensibly terrorist-related sanctions against a poor, weak
Soviet semisatellite and then refrain from taking similar
measures against other countries that are equally or more
guilty of supporting terrorism, but that happen to be richer,
stronger, or more favorably aligned politically, the appearance of expediency severely undermines the moral and political effectiveness of their counterterrorism efforts.

As the sanctions imposed in the Afghan case became
entangled with the broader issue of Western opposition
to the Soviet invasion of Afghanistan, their initial impact – the first time in history that flights had been collec-
tively suspended to a country because of its support for
aviation terrorism – dissipated. This politicization of the
sanctions was resented particularly in those European
countries whose national airlines actually had suspended
flights to Kabul – the United Kingdom, West Germany, and
France. Without necessarily feeling any less of a commitment to oppose the Soviet invasion, many involved officials
in these countries believed their airlines were being made to
bear the cost of a policy that had nothing to do with air
security or, for that matter, terrorism in general. This case
left a rather bad taste and has undoubtedly contributed to
the reluctance of certain members of the Seven to impose
aviation sanctions against other potential candidates.

The tendency to use counterterrorism strategies to
score political points in other areas is pernicious. Collective
action against state-supported terrorism derives political,
moral, and legal force from maintaining at least the appearance of a relatively impartial enforcement of international
norms. Although extraneous factors inevitably play a role
in the decision to adopt collective measures, to the extent

such measures become visibly corrupted by an overlay of unrelated issues they lose their force and, in so doing, also damage the potential for further action along the same lines. Moreover, from the opposite perspective, measures initially adopted to combat state-supported terrorism are not the most credible or effective means of promoting policy on broader political issues; if the democracies wish to show disapproval of Soviet policy in Afghanistan, for example, is it not more effective to do so explicitly and directly than under the guise of counterterrorism?

On the other hand, however, collective upholding of international counterterrorism standards cannot be overly mechanical. Efforts to promote the international rule of law inevitably take place against a variegated and constantly shifting political background, and consistency should not be confused with rigidity. Preservation of principle does not require the discarding of a sense of tactics and strategy. What is required is that the measures taken against any state supporter of terrorism be sufficiently strong, taking into account the gravity of the offense as well as all other relevant factors, to maintain the credibility of the counterterrorism stance of the governments adopting such measures.

An analogy from criminal law may help clarify the point. In a properly functioning legal system, a prosecutor, while never departing from the principle that a murder is a serious crime, may yet use quite different means of handling a murder case depending on its specific facts, public perceptions of it, prevailing attitudes of the judges and juries to be faced, and other relevant circumstances. In one instance, the most effective policy might be to seek the maximum penalty in a full-scale criminal trial. In another, such an approach might backfire, and a quiet plea bargain would be the best procedure. The wise prosecutor takes all such factors into account in deciding upon a strategy and also keeps in mind the effects of that strategy on the chances of future success in establishing precedents and maintaining the prestige and credibility of the state. There is all the more reason for a government seeking to bolster the international rule of law to take the analogous considerations into account in selecting an appropriate response to state-supported terrorism.

A Final Word

The political essence of the state-supported terrorist threat may be consistent, but its manifestations change over time, often in unexpected ways. Confident statements from Western leaders in the summer and fall of 1984 about the end of the skyjacking problem were followed almost immediately by a harrowing year of aviation terrorism that reached critical levels. Hostage-taking, too, had seemed under control by about 1984, but very shortly afterward resurfaced with a vengeance as perhaps the most emotionally and politically disturbing form of terrorism. The disproportionate terrorist threat to diplomatic personnel of the late 1970s and early 1980s, when diplomats accounted for as many as half of all the victims of terrorism, had drastically diminished by 1985 – only to be replaced by a new concern: diplomats as perpetrators, rather than targets, of terrorism.

This record gives little cause for complacency about the stability of current trends in international terrorism or about the West's ability to address future state-supported terrorism successfully without much hard work. Effective collective action against state supporters of terrorism will ultimately be based not on idealism or altruism, but on a healthy appreciation of the threats these states pose and of the dangers of disunity in the face of such threats. Such an appreciation, however, is not enough by itself. Effective action in this area does not just happen naturally, but requires an adequate understanding of the normative framework within which it occurs, a realistic perception of the relevant political and institutional contexts, and careful consideration of certain basic elements of a successful collective approach. The United States and its major democratic allies together have the potential to oppose the threat of state-supported terrorism effectively. Intelligent application of the lessons of past efforts is an essential step toward realizing that potential.

Appendix

Declarations of the Summit Seven on International Terrorism, 1978–1987

1. Bonn Economic Summit Conference
Joint Statement on International Terrorism,
July 17, 1978

The heads of state and government, concerned about terrorism and the taking of hostages, declare that their governments will intensify their joint efforts to combat international terrorism.

To this end, in cases where a country refuses extradition or prosecution of those who have hijacked an aircraft and/or do not return such aircraft, the heads of state and government are jointly resolved that their governments should take immediate action to cease all flights to that country.

At the same time, their governments will initiate action to halt all incoming flights from that country or from any country by the airlines of the country concerned. The heads of state and government urge other governments to join them in this commitment.

NOTE: Chancellor Helmut Schmidt read the joint statement during his remarks at the Bonn Stadt Theater at the conclusion of the Bonn Economic Summit Conference.

Source: Public Papers of the Presidents, Jimmy Carter, 1978.

2. Tokyo Economic Summit Conference

Joint Statement on Hijacking, Read As Part of
Prime Minister Ohira's Remarks to Reporters at the
Conclusion of the Conference, June 29, 1979

PRIME MINISTER OHIRA. Now, then, I would like to open the joint press conference.

To this summit there have gathered a great number of members of the press from Japan and from outside Japan, and for showing your interest in what goes on in the summit, I would like to express our appreciation. Because of security considerations, we may have caused you many inconveniences, but I hope you understand this.

Our conference during the past 2 days has been extremely useful, but in order for the fruit of our discussions to be appreciated in various parts of the world, much depends on you members of the press. I would be grateful for your cooperation.

I am going to shortly ask various heads of state and government to speak, but as the host, I would first like to give my overall evaluation.

In this summit we have welcomed three new members, of whom one is the first woman Prime Minister to the summit and the other is the youngest Prime Minister. The two new Prime Ministers have contributed much to the success of the conference with their charm and wisdom. The third new member is somewhat older, me, and I would refrain from making any comment.

Although nearly half of the members in this summit are new, I believe our summit has been able to create an extremely close human relation on the basis of the spirit of mutual support of the summit, which I believe is an important product of our endeavor.

This summit has been held as it was at the time when the attention of the world is focused on the oil problem. In order to respond to the situation, it has been said that our summit will be a failure unless bold and concrete measures are agreed upon.

Shortly the communiqué will be distributed to you, but from the viewpoint of both immediate measures and medium- and long-term points of view, I believe we have been able to reach concrete consensus that can respond to meet the expectations of the world.

As the Prime Minister of Japan, to give the specific goal of our effort to the year 1985 has taken considerable amount of courage, but recognizing the fact that we all live in a global community faced with the oil anxiety, and recognizing the need for placing our economy on a stable basis well into the future, I felt it was necessary for us to agree to that statement.

In areas other than oil, we have discussed questions such as inflation and employment, showing strong interest in protecting industrial democracies, from long-term and fundamental points of view. Although industrialized economies find ourselves in respective economic difficulties, the summit leaders have shown strong interest in the relationship with the developing nations. I have found this very encouraging. The old economies of the world are in the same boat. By sharing the new sense of responsibility and new sense of partnership, I would like to see the constructive relationship and cooperation be developed further.

Further, in the present summit, following up on what was taken up in the last summit in Bonn, we adopted a statement on air hijacking, which I will now read.

"All the heads of state and government" — excuse me, I take it back; I have the wrong text in front of me. [*Laughter*]

This is concerning the statement. At the request of heads of state and government who participated in the summit, I, in my capacity of chairman of the meeting, am pleased to make the following statement which concerns the declaration of air hijacking issued in Bonn in July 1978. I now read the statement.

"The heads of state and government express their pleasure with the broad support expressed by other states for the declaration on hijacking made at the Bonn Summit in July 1978.

"They noted that procedures for the prompt implementation of the declaration have been agreed upon and that to date enforcement measures under the declaration have not been necessary.

"They also noted with satisfaction the widespread adherence to the conventions dealing with unlawful interference with international civil aviation. Extensive support for these conventions and the Bonn declaration on hijacking reflects the acceptance by the international community as a whole of the principles expressed therein."

That is the statement.

Also, in the present summit, we have adopted a special statement on the question of refugees from Indochina,[1] which is another major fruit. Japan itself feels we must make our utmost contribution to the solution of this problem, and I would like to see that the statement be transmitted to other various countries and various international organizations and invite their further participation in international efforts on this question.

This has been an unprecedentedly important international event, but this Tokyo summit has now come to its safe and successful conclusion, and next year we have unanimously agreed to meet again in Italy. We look forward to our reunion in Italy.

And I would like to take this opportunity to express our heartfelt appreciation to all the people, both within and without Japan, who have supported this meeting. Because we have taken

------

[1][Issued on June 28 by the seven nations meeting at the Tokyo Economic Summit.]

STATEMENT ON INDOCHINESE REFUGEE CRISIS

The plight of refugees from Vietnam, Laos and Cambodia poses a humanitarian problem of historic proportions and constitutes a threat to the peace and stability of Southeast Asia. Given the tragedy and suffering which are taking place, the problem calls for an immediate and major response.

The Heads of State and Government call on Vietnam and other countries of Indochina to take urgent and effective measures so that the present human hardship and suffering are eliminated. They confirm the great importance they attach to the immediate cessation of the disorderly outflow of refugees without prejudice to the principles of free emigration and family reunification.

The governments represented will, as part of an international effort, significantly increase their contribution to Indochinese refugee relief and resettlement by making more funds available and by admitting more people, while taking into account the existing social and economic circumstances in each of their countries.

The Heads of State and Government request the Secretary-General of the United Nations to convene a conference as soon as possible with a view to attaining concrete and positive results. They extend full support to this objective and are ready to participate constructively in such a conference.

The Heads of State and Government call on all nations to join in addressing this pressing problem.

unexpected, unprecedentedly elaborate security measures in connection with the convening of this summit – and I know we have dealt inconveniences with many people, but because of their cooperation we have been able to successfully carry this conference. I thank all of these people concerned.

Thank you very much.

———

Source: Public Papers of the Presidents, Jimmy Carter, 1979.

3. Venice Economic Summit Conference

Statement on the Taking of Diplomatic Hostages, June 22, 1980

Gravely concerned by recent incidents of terrorism involving the taking of hostages and attacks on diplomatic and consular premises and personnel, the Heads of State and Government reaffirm their determination to deter and combat such acts. They note the completion of work on the International Convention Against the Taking of Hostages and call on all States to consider becoming parties to it as well as to the Convention on the Prevention and Punishment of Crimes Against Internationally Protected Persons of 1973.

The Heads of State and Government vigorously condemn the taking of hostages and the seizure of diplomatic and consular premises and personnel in contravention of the basic norms of international law and practice. The Heads of State and Government consider necessary that all Governments should adopt policies which will contribute to the attainment of this goal and to take appropriate measures to deny terrorists any benefits from such criminal acts. They also resolve to provide to one another's diplomatic and consular missions support and assistance in situations involving the seizure of diplomatic and consular establishments or personnel.

The Heads of State and Government recall that every State has the duty under international law to refrain from organizing, instigating, assisting or participating in terrorist acts in another State or acquiescing in organised activities within its territory

4. They were disturbed to note the ease with which terrorists move across international boundaries, and gain access to weapons, explosives, training and finance.

5. They viewed with serious concern the increasing involvement of states and governments in acts of terrorism, including the abuse of diplomatic immunity. They acknowledged the inviolability of diplomatic missions and other requirements of international law: but they emphasised the obligations which that law also entails.

6. Proposals which found support in the discussion included the following:
— closer co-operation and co-ordination between police and security organisations and other relevant authorities, especially in the exchange of information, intelligence and technical knowledge;
— scrutiny by each country of gaps in its national legislation which might be exploited by terrorists;
— use of the powers of the receiving state under the Vienna Convention in such matters as the size of diplomatic missions, and the number of buildings enjoying diplomatic immunity;
— action by each country to review the sale of weapons to states supporting terrorism;
— consultation and as far as possible co-operation over the expulsion or exclusion from their countries of known terrorists, including persons of diplomatic status involved in terrorism.

7. The Heads of State and Government recognised that this is a problem which affects all civilised states. They resolved to promote action through competent international organisations and among the international community as a whole to prevent and punish terrorist acts.

Source: Public Papers of the Presidents, Ronald Reagan, 1984.

directed towards the commission of such acts, and deplore in the strongest terms any breach of this duty.

NOTE: Prime Minister Francesco Cossiga of Italy, Chairman of the Conference, issued the statement to the press on behalf of the Conference participants.

As printed above, this item follows the text of the English translation made available by the White House. It was not issued as a White House press release.

Statement on Hijacking, June 22, 1980

The Heads of State and Government expressed their satisfaction at the broad support of the international community for the principles set out in the Bonn Declaration of July 1978 as well as in the international Conventions dealing with unlawful interference with civil aviation. The increasing adherence to these Conventions and the responsible attitude taken by States with respect to air-hijacking reflect the fact that these principles are being accepted by the international community as a whole.

The Heads of State and Government emphasize that hijacking remains a threat to international civil aviation and that there can be no relaxation of efforts to combat this threat. To this end they look forward to continuing cooperation with all other Governments.

NOTE: Prime Minister Francesco Cossiga of Italy, Chairman of the Conference, issued the statement to the press on behalf of the Conference participants.

As printed above, this item follows the text of the English translation made available by the White House. It was not issued as a White House press release.

Source: Public Papers of the Presidents, Jimmy Carter, 1980.

4. Ottawa Economic Summit Conference
Statement on Terrorism, July 20, 1981

1. The Heads of State and Government, seriously concerned about the active support given to international terrorism through the supply of money and arms to terrorist groups, and about the sanctuary and training offered terrorists, as well as the continuation of acts of violence and terrorism such as aircraft hijacking, hostage-taking and attacks against diplomatic and consular personnel and premises, reaffirm their determination vigorously to combat such flagrant violations of international law. Emphasizing that all countries are threatened by acts of terrorism in disregard of fundamental human rights, they resolve to strengthen and broaden action within the international community to prevent and punish such acts.

2. The Heads of State and Government view with particular concern the recent hijacking incidents which threaten the safety of international civil aviation. They recall and reaffirm the principles set forth in the 1978 Bonn Declaration and note that there are several hijackings which have not been resolved by certain states in conformity with their obligations under international law. They call upon the governments concerned to discharge their obligations promptly and thereby contribute to the safety of international civil aviation.

3. The Heads of State and Government are convinced that, in the case of the hijacking of a Pakistan International Airlines aircraft in March, the conduct of the Babrak Karmal government of Afghanistan, both during the incident and subsequently in giving refuge to the hijackers, was and is in flagrant breach of its international obligations under the Hague Convention to which Afghanistan is a party, and constitutes a serious threat to air safety. Consequently the Heads of State and Government propose to suspend all flights to and from Afghanistan in implementation of the Bonn Declaration unless Afghanistan immediately takes steps to comply with its obligations. Furthermore, they call upon all states which share their concern for air safety to take appropriate action to persuade Afghanistan to honour its obligations.

4. Recalling the Venice Statement on the Taking of Diplomatic Hostages, the Heads of State and Government approve continued cooperation in the event of attacks on diplomatic and con-

sular establishments or personnel of any of their governments. They undertake that in the event of such incidents, their governments will immediately consult on an appropriate response. Moreover, they resolve that any state which directly aids and abets the commission of terrorist acts condemned in the Venice Statement, should face a prompt international response. It was agreed to exchange information on terrorist threats and activities, and to explore cooperative measures for dealing with and countering acts of terrorism, for promoting more effective implementation of existing anti-terrorist conventions, and for securing wider adherence to them.

Conference Participants

President Reagan, Prime Minister Trudeau, President François Mitterrand of France, Chancellor Helmut Schmidt of the Federal Republic of Germany, Prime Minister Zenko Suzuki of Japan, Prime Minister Margaret Thatcher of the United Kingdom, Prime Minister Giovanni Spadolini of Italy, and Gaston Thorn, President of the Commission of the European Communities.

Source: Public Papers of the Presidents, Ronald Reagan, 1981.

5. London Economic Summit Conference
*Declaration on International Terrorism,
June 9, 1984*

1. The Heads of State and Government discussed the pr international terrorism.

2. They noted that hijacking and kidnapping h since the Declarations of Bonn (1978), Venice (1980) (1981) as a result of improved security measures, bv ism had developed other techniques, sometimes with traffic in drugs.

3. They expressed their resolve to combat th' possible means, strengthening existing measur effective new ones.

6. Tokyo Economic Summit
Statement on International Terrorism, May 5, 1986

1. We, the Heads of State or Government of seven major democracies and the representatives of the European Community, assembled here in Tokyo, strongly reaffirm our condemnation of international terrorism in all its forms, of its accomplices and of those, including governments, who sponsor or support it. We abhor the increase in the level of such terrorism since our last meeting, and in particular its blatant and cynical use as an instrument of government policy. Terrorism has no justification. It spreads only by the use of contemptible means, ignoring the values of human life, freedom and dignity. It must be fought relentlessly and without compromise.

2. Recognizing that the continuing fight against terrorism is a task which the international community as a whole has to undertake, we pledge ourselves to make maximum efforts to fight against that scourge. Terrorism must be fought effectively through determined, tenacious, discreet and patient action combining national measures with international cooperation. Therefore, we urge all like-minded nations to collaborate with us, particularly in such international fora as the United Nations, the International Civil Aviation Organization and the International Maritime Organization, drawing on their expertise to improve and extend countermeasures against terrorism and those who sponsor or support it.

3. We, the Heads of State or Government, agree to intensify the exchange of information in relevant fora on threats and potential threats emanating from terrorist activities and those who sponsor or support them, and on ways to prevent them.

4. We specify the following as measures open to any government concerned to deny to international terrorists the opportunity and the means to carry out their aims, and to identify and deter those who perpetrate such terrorism. We have decided to apply these measures within the framework of international law and in our own jurisdictions in respect of any state which is clearly involved in sponsoring or supporting international terrorism, and in particular of Libya, until such time as the state concerned abandons its complicity in, or support for, such terrorism. These measures are:

—refusal to export arms to states which sponsor or support terrorism;

—strict limits on the size of the diplomatic and consular missions and other official bodies abroad of states which engage in such activities, control of travel of members of such missions and bodies, and, where appropriate, radical reductions in, or even the closure of, such missions and bodies;

—denial of entry to all persons, including diplomatic personnel, who have been expelled or excluded from one of our states on suspicion of involvement in international terrorism or who have been convicted of such a terrorist offence;

—improved extradition procedures within due process of domestic law for bringing to trial those who have perpetrated such acts of terrorism;

—stricter immigration and visa requirements and procedures in respect of nationals of states which sponsor or support terrorism;

—the closest possible bilateral and multilateral cooperation between police and security organizations and other relevant authorities in the fight against terrorism.

Each of us is committed to work in the appropriate international bodies to which we belong to ensure that similar measures are accepted and acted upon by as many other governments as possible.

5. We will maintain close cooperation in furthering the objectives of this statement and in considering further measures. We agree to make the 1978 Bonn Declaration more effective in dealing with all forms of terrorism affecting civil aviation. We are ready to promote bilaterally and multilaterally further actions to be taken in international organizations or fora competent to fight against international terrorism in any of its forms.

Source: Weekly Compilation of Presidential Documents, vol. 22, no. 19 (May 12, 1986).

directed towards the commission of such acts, and deplore in the strongest terms any breach of this duty.

NOTE: Prime Minister Francesco Cossiga of Italy, Chairman of the Conference, issued the statement to the press on behalf of the Conference participants.

As printed above, this item follows the text of the English translation made available by the White House. It was not issued as a White House press release.

Statement on Hijacking, June 22, 1980

The Heads of State and Government expressed their satisfaction at the broad support of the international community for the principles set out in the Bonn Declaration of July 1978 as well as in the international Conventions dealing with unlawful interference with civil aviation. The increasing adherence to these Conventions and the responsible attitude taken by States with respect to air-hijacking reflect the fact that these principles are being accepted by the international community as a whole.

The Heads of State and Government emphasize that hijacking remains a threat to international civil aviation and that there can be no relaxation of efforts to combat this threat. To this end they look forward to continuing cooperation with all other Governments.

NOTE: Prime Minister Francesco Cossiga of Italy, Chairman of the Conference, issued the statement to the press on behalf of the Conference participants.

As printed above, this item follows the text of the English translation made available by the White House. It was not issued as a White House press release.

Source: Public Papers of the Presidents, Jimmy Carter, 1980.

4. Ottawa Economic Summit Conference
Statement on Terrorism, July 20, 1981

1. The Heads of State and Government, seriously concerned about the active support given to international terrorism through the supply of money and arms to terrorist groups, and about the sanctuary and training offered terrorists, as well as the continuation of acts of violence and terrorism such as aircraft hijacking, hostage-taking and attacks against diplomatic and consular personnel and premises, reaffirm their determination vigorously to combat such flagrant violations of international law. Emphasizing that all countries are threatened by acts of terrorism in disregard of fundamental human rights, they resolve to strengthen and broaden action within the international community to prevent and punish such acts.

2. The Heads of State and Government view with particular concern the recent hijacking incidents which threaten the safety of international civil aviation. They recall and reaffirm the principles set forth in the 1978 Bonn Declaration and note that there are several hijackings which have not been resolved by certain states in conformity with their obligations under international law. They call upon the governments concerned to discharge their obligations promptly and thereby contribute to the safety of international civil aviation.

3. The Heads of State and Government are convinced that, in the case of the hijacking of a Pakistan International Airlines aircraft in March, the conduct of the Babrak Karmal government of Afghanistan, both during the incident and subsequently in giving refuge to the hijackers, was and is in flagrant breach of its international obligations under the Hague Convention to which Afghanistan is a party, and constitutes a serious threat to air safety. Consequently the Heads of State and Government propose to suspend all flights to and from Afghanistan in implementation of the Bonn Declaration unless Afghanistan immediately takes steps to comply with its obligations. Furthermore, they call upon all states which share their concern for air safety to take appropriate action to persuade Afghanistan to honour its obligations.

4. Recalling the Venice Statement on the Taking of Diplomatic Hostages, the Heads of State and Government approve continued cooperation in the event of attacks on diplomatic and con-

sular establishments or personnel of any of their governments. They undertake that in the event of such incidents, their governments will immediately consult on an appropriate response. Moreover, they resolve that any state which directly aids and abets the commission of terrorist acts condemned in the Venice Statement, should face a prompt international response. It was agreed to exchange information on terrorist threats and activities, and to explore cooperative measures for dealing with and countering acts of terrorism, for promoting more effective implementation of existing anti-terrorist conventions, and for securing wider adherence to them.

Conference Participants

President Reagan, Prime Minister Trudeau, President François Mitterrand of France, Chancellor Helmut Schmidt of the Federal Republic of Germany, Prime Minister Zenko Suzuki of Japan, Prime Minister Margaret Thatcher of the United Kingdom, Prime Minister Giovanni Spadolini of Italy, and Gaston Thorn, President of the Commission of the European Communities.

Source: Public Papers of the Presidents, Ronald Reagan, 1981.

5. London Economic Summit Conference

Declaration on International Terrorism,
June 9, 1984

1. The Heads of State and Government discussed the problem of international terrorism.

2. They noted that hijacking and kidnapping had declined since the Declarations of Bonn (1978), Venice (1980) and Ottawa (1981) as a result of improved security measures, but that terrorism had developed other techniques, sometimes in association with traffic in drugs.

3. They expressed their resolve to combat this threat by every possible means, strengthening existing measures and developing effective new ones.

4. They were disturbed to note the ease with which terrorists move across international boundaries, and gain access to weapons, explosives, training and finance.

5. They viewed with serious concern the increasing involvement of states and governments in acts of terrorism, including the abuse of diplomatic immunity. They acknowledged the inviolability of diplomatic missions and other requirements of international law: but they emphasised the obligations which that law also entails.

6. Proposals which found support in the discussion included the following:

- closer co-operation and co-ordination between police and security organisations and other relevant authorities, especially in the exchange of information, intelligence and technical knowledge;
- scrutiny by each country of gaps in its national legislation which might be exploited by terrorists;
- use of the powers of the receiving state under the Vienna Convention in such matters as the size of diplomatic missions, and the number of buildings enjoying diplomatic immunity;
- action by each country to review the sale of weapons to states supporting terrorism;
- consultation and as far as possible co-operation over the expulsion or exclusion from their countries of known terrorists, including persons of diplomatic status involved in terrorism.

7. The Heads of State and Government recognised that this is a problem which affects all civilised states. They resolved to promote action through competent international organisations and among the international community as a whole to prevent and punish terrorist acts.

_____

Source: Public Papers of the Presidents, Ronald Reagan, 1984.

6. Tokyo Economic Summit
Statement on International Terrorism, May 5, 1986

1. We, the Heads of State or Government of seven major democracies and the representatives of the European Community, assembled here in Tokyo, strongly reaffirm our condemnation of international terrorism in all its forms, of its accomplices and of those, including governments, who sponsor or support it. We abhor the increase in the level of such terrorism since our last meeting, and in particular its blatant and cynical use as an instrument of government policy. Terrorism has no justification. It spreads only by the use of contemptible means, ignoring the values of human life, freedom and dignity. It must be fought relentlessly and without compromise.

2. Recognizing that the continuing fight against terrorism is a task which the international community as a whole has to undertake, we pledge ourselves to make maximum efforts to fight against that scourge. Terrorism must be fought effectively through determined, tenacious, discreet and patient action combining national measures with international cooperation. Therefore, we urge all like-minded nations to collaborate with us, particularly in such international fora as the United Nations, the International Civil Aviation Organization and the International Maritime Organization, drawing on their expertise to improve and extend countermeasures against terrorism and those who sponsor or support it.

3. We, the Heads of State or Government, agree to intensify the exchange of information in relevant fora on threats and potential threats emanating from terrorist activities and those who sponsor or support them, and on ways to prevent them.

4. We specify the following as measures open to any government concerned to deny to international terrorists the opportunity and the means to carry out their aims, and to identify and deter those who perpetrate such terrorism. We have decided to apply these measures within the framework of international law and in our own jurisdictions in respect of any state which is clearly involved in sponsoring or supporting international terrorism, and in particular of Libya, until such time as the state concerned abandons its complicity in, or support for, such terrorism. These measures are:

— refusal to export arms to states which sponsor or support terrorism;

— strict limits on the size of the diplomatic and consular missions and other official bodies abroad of states which engage in such activities, control of travel of members of such missions and bodies, and, where appropriate, radical reductions in, or even the closure of, such missions and bodies;

— denial of entry to all persons, including diplomatic personnel, who have been expelled or excluded from one of our states on suspicion of involvement in international terrorism or who have been convicted of such a terrorist offence;

— improved extradition procedures within due process of domestic law for bringing to trial those who have perpetrated such acts of terrorism;

— stricter immigration and visa requirements and procedures in respect of nationals of states which sponsor or support terrorism;

— the closest possible bilateral and multilateral cooperation between police and security organizations and other relevant authorities in the fight against terrorism.

Each of us is committed to work in the appropriate international bodies to which we belong to ensure that similar measures are accepted and acted upon by as many other governments as possible.

5. We will maintain close cooperation in furthering the objectives of this statement and in considering further measures. We agree to make the 1978 Bonn Declaration more effective in dealing with all forms of terrorism affecting civil aviation. We are ready to promote bilaterally and multilaterally further actions to be taken in international organizations or fora competent to fight against international terrorism in any of its forms.

Source: Weekly Compilation of Presidential Documents, vol. 22, no. 19 (May 12, 1986).

7. Venice Economic Summit

Statement on Terrorism, June 9, 1987

Terrorism

We, the heads of state or government of seven major democracies and the representatives of the European Community assembled here in Venice, profoundly aware of our peoples' concern at the threat posed by terrorism:

• Reaffirm our commitment to the statements on terrorism made at previous summits, in Bonn, Venice, Ottawa, London and Tokyo;

• Resolutely condemn all forms of terrorism, including aircraft hijackings and hostage-taking, and reiterate our belief that whatever its motives, terrorism has no justification;

• Confirm the commitment of each of us to the principle of making no concessions to terrorists or their sponsors;

• Remain resolved to apply, in respect of any state clearly involved in sponsoring or supporting international terrorism, effective measures within the framework of international law and in our own jurisdictions;

• Welcome the progress made in international cooperation against terrorism since we last met in Tokyo in May 1986, and in particular the initiative taken by France and Germany to convene in May in Paris a meeting of ministers of nine countries, who are responsible for counterterrorism;

• Reaffirm our determination to combat terrorism both through national measures and through international cooperation among ourselves and with others, when appropriate, and therefore renew our appeal to all like-minded countries to consolidate and extend international cooperation in all appropriate fora;

• Will continue our efforts to improve the safety of travelers. We welcome improvements in airport and maritime security, and encourage the work of I.C.A.O. and I.M.O. in this regard. Each of us will continue to monitor closely the activities of airlines which raise security problems. The heads of state or government have decided on measures, annexed to this statement, to make the 1978 Bonn Declaration more effective in dealing with all forms of terrorism affecting civil aviation;

• Commit ourselves to support the rule of law in bringing terrorists to justice. Each of us pledges increased cooperation in the relevant fora and within the framework of domestic and international law on the investigation, apprehension and prosecution of terrorists. In particular we reaffirm the principle established by relevant international conventions of trying or extraditing, according to national laws and those international conventions, those who have perpetrated acts of terrorism.

Annex

The heads of state or government recall that in their Tokyo statement on international terrorism they agreed to make the 1978 Bonn Declaration more effective in dealing with all forms of terrorism affecting civil aviation. To this end, in cases where a country refuses extradition or prosecution of those who have committed offenses described in the Montreal Convention for the Suppression of Unlawful Acts against the Safety of Civil Aviation and/or does not return the aircraft involved, the heads of state or government are jointly resolved that their Governments shall take immediate action to cease flights to that country as stated in the Bonn Declaration.

At the same time, their governments will initiate action to halt incoming flights from that country or from any country by the airlines of the country concerned as stated in the Bonn Declaration.

The heads of state or government intend also to extend the Bonn Declaration in due time to cover any future relevant amendment to the above convention or any other aviation conventions relating to the extradition or prosecution of the offenders.

The heads of state or government urge other governments to join them in this commitment.

Source: "Venice Statements on East-West Relations, Terrorism and Persian Gulf," *New York Times*, June 10, 1987.

Notes

Introduction

1. "State-supported" is used here to refer to passive support, such as the granting of sanctuary to terrorists, as well as more active state involvement in terrorist acts.

2. U.S. Department of State, *American Foreign Policy: Current Documents, 1981* (Washington, D.C.: Government Printing Office [GPO], 1984), 395.

3. Statement by the Under Secretary of State for Management (Richard T. Kennedy) before the Senate Foreign Relations Committee, June 10, 1981, in ibid., 398.

4. *Weekly Compilation of Presidential Documents* 20 (January 30, 1984), 93.

5. U.S. Department of State, *American Foreign Policy: Current Documents 1985* (Washington, D.C.: GPO, 1986), 274.

6. L. Paul Bremer III, "Practical Measures for Dealing with Terrorism," talk delivered at the Discover Conference on Terrorism in a Technological World, January 22, 1987.

7. Public Law No. 99-399, 99 Stat. 853, sec. 701.

8. *New York Times*, June 10, 1987, p. A10.

Chapter 1

1. Benjamin Netanyahu, "Defining Terrorism," in Benjamin

Netanyahu, ed., *Terrorism: How the West Can Win* (New York: Farrar, Straus & Giroux, 1986), 9.

2. This cumulative process, incidentally, continues today, as discussions are under way in the relevant specialized UN agencies on placing new forms of terrorism, such as maritime terrorism and attacks at international airports, under similar regimes.

3. "The Contracting State in the territory of which the alleged offender is found shall, if it does not extradite him, be obliged, without exception whatsoever and whether or not the offence was committed in its territory, to submit the case to its competent authorities for the purpose of prosecution" (Art. 7); 22 U.S.T. 1641, T.I.A.S. 7192.

4. G.A. Res. 2551 (XXIV), 24 U.N. G.A.O.R., U.N. Doc. A/RES/2551 (XXIV), January 6, 1970.

5. ICAO Resolutions A17-1 through A17-24, June 16–30, 1970, reprinted in *International Legal Materials* 9 (1970): 1275.

6. Resolution A17-3 in ibid., p. 1276.

7. G.A. Res. 2645 (XXV), 25 U.N. G.A.O.R., U.N. Doc. A/RES/2645 (XXV), November 30, 1970.

8. ICAO Doc. 8923-C/998, reprinted in *International Legal Materials* 9 (1970): 1286 (emphasis added).

9. See Kevin Chamberlain, "Collective Suspension of Air Services with States Which Harbour Hijackers," *International and Comparative Law Quarterly* 32 (1983): 616, 618.

10. Other proposals included a joint British-Swiss proposal to amend the Convention on International Civil Aviation (Chicago Convention), 61 Stat. 1180, T.I.A.S. 1591, December 7, 1944, to provide the ICAO Council with the power to determine that a contracting state had violated its obligations concerning the handling of a skyjacking or aircraft sabotage incident and consequently to require all contracting states to deny access to their airspace to any airline of the defaulting state, and a French proposal to amend the Chicago Convention to incorporate the substantive provisions of the Hague Convention without providing any provisions for new enforcement sanctions. See Chamberlain, "Collective Suspension," 622–23.

11. Ibid., 625–26.

12. These include "perform[ing] an act of violence against a person on board an aircraft if that act is likely to endanger the safety of that aircraft; . . . destroy[ing] an aircraft in service or

caus[ing] damage to such an aircraft which renders it incapable of flight or which is likely to endanger its safety in flight; or . . . plac-[ing] or caus[ing] to be placed on an aircraft in service, by any means whatsoever, a device or substance which is likely to destroy that aircraft, or to cause damage to it which renders it incapable of flight, or to cause damage to it which is likely to endanger its safety in flight . . . " (Art. 1[1]); 24 U.S.T. 564, T.I.A.S. 7570.

13. See Robert G. Bell, "The U.S. Response to Terrorism against International Civil Aviation," *Orbis* 19 (1975–76): 1333–34.

14. 27 U.S.T. 3949, T.I.A.S. 8413.

15. Those persons were essentially foreign diplomats, as well as certain other limited categories – visiting heads of state, for example.

16. In particular, Article 3 provided: "In any case, it is the exclusive responsibility of the state under whose jurisdiction or protection such persons are located to determine the nature of the acts and decide whether the standards of this convention are applicable."

17. The Vienna Convention, April 18, 1961, 23 U.S.T. 3227, T.I.A.S. 7502; on the OAS Convention, see Michael C. Wood, "The Convention on the Prevention and Punishment of Crimes against Internationally Protected Persons, Including Diplomatic Agents," *International and Comparative Law Quarterly* 23 (1974): 793.

18. U.N. Doc. A/C.6/L.951/Rev.1, quoted in ibid., 795.

19. 28 U.S.T. 1975, T.I.A.S. 8532.

20. Vienna Convention on Diplomatic Relations, see note 17 above; Vienna Convention on Consular Relations, April 24, 1963, 21 U.S.T. 77, T.I.A.S. 6820.

21. Department of State treaty files.

22. John W. McDonald, Jr., "The United Nations Convention against the Taking of Hostages: The Inside Story," *Terrorism: An International Journal* 6 (1983), 546.

23. U.N. G.A.O.R. Supp. No. 46 (A/3443), 1979, pp. 245–47, U.N. Doc. A/RES/34/146.

24. See Abraham D. Sofaer, "Terrorism and the Law," *Foreign Affairs* 64 (1986), 916.

25. See McDonald, "The United Nations Convention against the Taking of Hostages," 549. "Anti-Entebbe" refers to the 1976

Israeli raid on Entebbe Airport in Uganda to free hostages from a hijacked airliner.

26. A clause of this sort is, however, a common feature of bilateral extradition treaties. Of course, in light of Article 8 a state failing to extradite under this provision would be bound to submit the alleged hostage-taker's case to its own authorities for prosecution.

27. The weakness of this dispute settlement mechanism is discussed by Robert Rosenstock, a key U.S. participant in the negotiation of the Hostages Convention, in "International Convention against the Taking of Hostages: Another International Community Step against Terrorism," *Journal of International Law and Policy* 9 (1980): 187.

28. The Soviet delegate had been notably obstructive during the negotiation of the convention text, reflecting obvious Soviet dislike of the concept, though the USSR did not go as far as formally opposing the adoption of the convention by the General Assembly. McDonald, "The United Nations Convention against the Taking of Hostages," 556–57. The USSR did become a party to the Hostages Convention in June 1987.

29. S.C. Res. 579, 40 U.N. SCOR (2637th mtg.), 24–25, U.N. Doc. S/17,685 (1985).

30. A similar though somewhat less extensive structure of privileges and immunities exists for consular officers by virtue of the Vienna Convention on Consular Relations, supplemented in some cases by bilateral agreements. For purposes of the present discussion, however, the distinctions are irrelevant.

31. This immunity, however, subsists only until the diplomatic agent leaves the receiving state upon expiry of his tour of duty (Art. 39[2]). The receiving state would not be legally barred from prosecuting a person who later returned to that state in a nondiplomatic capacity for acts committed during a previous sojourn when the person had had diplomatic immunity, unless the acts in question were committed "in the exercise of his functions as a member of the mission" – which presumably did not include committing terrorist crimes.

32. See Frank Brenchley, *Diplomatic Immunities and State-sponsored Terrorism* (London: Institute for the Study of Conflict, Conflict Studies Series No. 164, 1984), 20. Article 31(4) makes clear that the sending state preserves criminal jurisdiction over

its own diplomatic agent for acts committed in the receiving state. In cases of terrorist abuse of diplomatic privileges and immunities, however, the sending state is hardly likely to exercise such jurisdiction in any meaningful way.

33. S. Res. 74, 100th Cong., 1st sess., 2–3.

34. See Testimony of Acting State Department Legal Adviser McGovern before the Senate Judiciary Committee, Subcommittee on Security and Terrorism, July 24, 1984, pp. 6–7 (copy in State Department files); Brenchley, *Diplomatic Immunities*, 21–23.

35. League of Nations Doc. C.546.M383.1937.V (1937).

36. G.A. Res. 2625, 25 U.N. G.A.O.R. Supp. (no. 28), 121, U.N. Doc. A/8028 (1970).

37. See John Dugard, "International Terrorism: Problems of Definition," *International Affairs* 50 (1974): 70–74.

38. G.A. Res. 40/61, 40 U.N. G.A.O.R. Supp. (no. 53), 301, U.N. Doc. A/40/53 (1985).

39. See Edward Mickolus, *Transnational Terrorism: A Chronology of Events, 1968-1979* (Westport, Conn.: Greenwood Press, 1980), 153ff. This was, of course, far from the first outbreak of political terrorism in world history, but the early 1970s did mark the initial emergence of terrorism as an international political issue in the postwar period.

40. Noemi Gal-Or, *International Cooperation to Suppress Terrorism* (New York: St. Martin's Press, 1985), 83.

41. Quoted in W. Tapley Bennett, "U.S. Initiatives in the United Nations to Combat International Terrorism," *International Lawyer* 7 (1973): 753.

42. U.N. Doc. A/C.6/L.850 (1972).

43. See *International Legal Materials* 12 (1972): 220.

44. Gal-Or, *International Cooperation*, 84.

45. *Report on International Terrorism*, Council of Europe Document No. 3201, at 6 (October 18, 1972), quoted in Gal-Or, *International Cooperation*, 209. See also ibid., 218–20.

46. Quoted in Gal-Or, *International Cooperation*, 219.

47. Bennett, "U.S. Initiatives," 758. Ambassador Bennett was a member of the U.S. delegation to the 27th UN General Assembly and represented the United States in the Legal Committee (ibid., 752).

48. See the following in Gal-Or, *International Cooperation*: COE – chapters 6–10; EC – 220–21, 327–28; and NATO – 75.

Chapter 2

1. *Public Report of the Vice President's Task Force on Combatting Terrorism* (Washington, D.C.: GPO, 1986), 12.

2. See the excellent discussion of this problem, focusing particularly on the shortcomings in this regard of NATO and the EC, in Parker W. Borg, *International Terrorism: Breaking the Cycle of Violence*, Occasional Paper No. 8 (Washington, D.C.: Center for the Study of Foreign Affairs, Foreign Service Institute, U.S. Department of State, June 1987), 18–20.

3. Guido Garavoglia, "From Rambouillet to Williamsburg: A Historical Assessment," in Cesare Merlini, ed., *Economic Summits and Western Decision-Making* (New York: St. Martin's Press, 1984), 5.

4. Ibid., 16. For a particularly relevant and quite negative view of this formalization trend, see the interview with former French President Valéry Giscard d'Estaing in *Le Monde*, June 6, 1987, p. 1.

5. Robert D. Putnam and Nicholas Bayne, *Hanging Together: The Seven-Power Summits* (Cambridge, Mass.: Harvard University Press, 1984), 94.

6. Joint Statement of the Heads of State and Government on International Terrorism, Bonn Summit Meeting, July 17, 1978, in *Department of State Bulletin* 78 (September 1978), 5.

7. U.S. Department of State, Office for Combatting Terrorism, *Terrorist Skyjackings* (1982), 2. For purposes of these statistics, a "terrorist" skyjacking was defined as "[t]he seizure of an airplane through the use or threat of violence for political purposes by individuals or groups" (ibid., i).

8. Ibid., 2.

9. Ibid., 4.

10. Ibid., 19.

11. Remarks by the President (Carter) at the Conclusion of the Economic Summit Conference, Bonn, July 17, 1978 in U.S. Department of State, *American Foreign Policy: Current Documents, 1977–1980* (Washington, D.C.: GPO, 1981), 338.

12. Ibid.

13. *Department of State Bulletin* 78 (September 1978): 5.

14. Ibid.

15. Joint Statement on Hijacking, June 29, 1979, reprinted in *Public Papers of the Presidents*, Jimmy Carter, 1979.

16. Statement by the Heads of State and Government on Hijacking, Venice Summit Meeting, June 22, 1980, *Department of State Bulletin* 80 (August 1980): 7.

17. See Department of State, *Terrorist Skyjackings*, 2. In the year following the issuance of the Bonn Declaration, 34 other states had expressed support for it; another 43 had indicated approval of its underlying principle while stopping short of an actual expression of support for the declaration itself (information in Department of State files). Between 1978 and 1980 over 25 states signed or became parties to the Hague Convention; the same number signed or became parties to the Montreal Convention (Department of State treaty records).

18. See Department of State, *Terrorist Skyjackings*, 20.

19. Statement by the Heads of State and Government on Terrorism, Ottawa Summit Meeting, July 21, 1981, *Department of State Bulletin* 81 (August 1981): 16.

20. Ibid. The aviation sanctions against Afghanistan are discussed in more detail in chapter 3.

21. This declaration devoted particular attention to the problems of state-sponsored terrorism and abuse of diplomatic privileges and immunities. Declaration of the Heads of State and Government on International Terrorism, London Summit Meeting, June 9, 1984, *Department of State Bulletin* 84 (August 1984): 4. For further discussion see pp. 39–41 below.

22. U.S. Department of Transportation, Federal Aviation Administration, Office of Civil Aviation Security, *U.S. and Foreign Registered Aircraft Hijackings* (1985), 98–118.

23. Ibid., 118–120.

24. Remarks by President Reagan, Kansas City, Missouri, October 21, 1984 in U.S. Department of State, *American Foreign Policy: Current Documents 1984* (Washington, D.C.: GPO, 1986), 308.

25. For the July and December 1984 incidents, see U.S. Department of State, *Patterns of Global Terrorism: 1984* (1985), 26 and 28, respectively; for the June and November 1985 incidents, see U.S. Department of State, *Patterns of Global Terrorism: 1985* (1986), 19 and 12, respectively. The Egyptair hijacking came to a tragic close when Egyptian commandos stormed the airplane; some 60 people died in the rescue effort.

26. Statement of the Heads of State and Government on Ter-

rorism, Tokyo Summit Meeting, May 5, 1986, *Department of State Bulletin* 86 (July 1986): 5 (emphasis added).

27. Between January 1968 and July 1982, records show a total of 53 explosions aboard aircraft, not all of which would be classifiable as sabotage (U.S. Department of Transportation, Federal Aviation Administration, Office of Civil Aviation Security, *Explosions Aboard Aircraft*, 1985, pp. 4–11); during the same period, 684 skyjacking attempts were recorded (Department of State, *Terrorist Skyjackings*, 1).

28. For the 1985 incidents, see Department of State, *Patterns of Global Terrorism: 1985*, p. 37; for the TWA incident, see *New York Times*, April 3, 1986, p. 1.

29. *New York Times*, September 16, 1986, p. 9.

30. Statement on Terrorism, June 9, 1987, *Department of State Bulletin* 87 (August 1987): 3.

31. Of course, aircraft hijacking itself is in a sense a subcategory of hostage-taking: the taking of hostages who happen to be aboard an aircraft in flight. It is not the capture of the airplane itself, but rather of the people on it, that gives skyjacking its effect. But these two forms of terrorism have been treated distinctly in the efforts of the Seven as well as of other segments of the international community, so that it is appropriate to follow that practice in the discussion here.

32. U.S. Department of State, *International Terrorism: Hostage Seizures* (1983), 2, 5.

33. Ibid., 23.

34. The initiative for this declaration reportedly came from the United States. Putnam and Bayne, *Hanging Together*, 131.

35. *Department of State Bulletin* 80 (August 1980): 1–8.

36. U.S. Department of State, *Terrorist Incidents Involving Diplomats* (1980), 1.

37. Ibid.

38. Ibid., 6.

39. Ibid., 3, 7.

40. U.S. Department of State, *International Terrorism: Hostage Seizures*, 24.

41. Ibid., 14, 15.

42. Ibid. The April 1980 incident ended when British special forces stormed the embassy, killing five of the six terrorists and rescuing all remaining hostages.

43. Putnam and Bayne, *Hanging Together*, 131. Other state-

ments issued at the Venice meeting addressed Afghanistan, refugees and hijacking. See *Department of State Bulletin* 80 (March 1980): 7.

44. Ibid.

45. Copy of announcement in State Department files. Among the more notorious incidents of international terrorism directed against diplomats in 1982 and 1983 were the assassination of U.S. assistant military attaché Lt. Col. Charles Ray in Paris in January 1982; the assassination of Israeli diplomat Yacov Barsimantov in Paris in April 1982; the car bombing of the French embassy in Beirut in May 1982, in which 12 people were killed and dozens injured; the assassination attempt against Israeli Ambassador Shlomo Argov in London in June 1982, which left the ambassador critically wounded; the assassination of Turkish Ambassador Galip Balkar in Belgrade in March 1983; the suicide vehicle bombing of the U.S. embassy in Beirut in April 1983, resulting in 57 deaths and numerous injuries; and the bombings of the U.S. and French embassies in Kuwait in December 1983 (five persons were killed in the U.S. embassy bombing). U.S. Department of State, *Patterns of International Terrorism: 1982*, pp. 17–18; *Patterns of Global Terrorism: 1983*, pp. 21–26.

46. U.S. Department of State, *Patterns of Global Terrorism: 1985*, p. 3.

47. Declaration on International Terrorism, *Department of State Bulletin* 84 (August 1984): 4.

48. See pp. 39–41 below for a discussion of the London declaration and the problem of terrorist abuse of diplomatic privileges and immunities.

49. U.S. Department of State, *Patterns of Global Terrorism: 1985*, p. 3.

50. Summit Statement on Terrorism, *Department of State Bulletin* 86 (July 1986): 5.

51. U.S. Department of State, *Patterns of Global Terrorism: 1983* (1984), 6; U.S. Department of State, *Patterns of Global Terrorism: 1984*, p. 18.

52. U.S. Department of State, *Patterns of Global Terrorism: 1985*, p. 28.

53. *New York Times*, June 10, 1987, p. A10.

54. See *The Times* (London), May 2, 1984, p. 5.

55. *The Times* (London), June 11, 1984, p. 4.

56. Press Briefing by the Honorable George P. Shultz, U.S.

Secretary of State, London, England, June 9, 1984, Department of State Press Release No. 155, June 21, 1984, pp. 4, 6.

57. Letter of November 2, 1984, from Assistant Secretary of State for Legislative and Intergovernmental Affairs W. Tapley Bennett, Jr., to Senator Arlen Specter (R-Pa.).

58. Chronology of terrorist incidents, *Department of State Bulletin* 87 (February 1987): 75.

59. Ibid. The latter incident is discussed in detail in chapter 3.

60. *Department of State Bulletin* 86 (June 1986): 1. This incident is discussed in detail in chapter 3.

61. *The Times* (London), April 28, 1986, p. 5.

62. Ibid., April 5, 1986, p. 6.

63. Tokyo Economic Summit, Secretary Shultz's News Briefing, May 5, 1986, *Department of State Bulletin* 86 (July 1986): 6.

64. *Facts on File* 46 (May 9, 1986), 329.

65. *The Economist*, April 11, 1987, p. 34.

66. *The Times* (London), February 6, 1987, p. 6.

67. FBIS Western Europe Report, 5 February 1987, p. K1, "Government Opposes 'Seven' Meeting on Terrorism," Paris Domestic Service (in French), 1300 GMT, 5 February 1987.

68. *Washington Post*, February 6, 1987, p. A18.

69. *The Times* (London), February 7, 1987, p. 1.

70. *Washington Post*, May 29, 1987, p. A27.

71. *Le Monde* described the gathering as a "personal success of M. Charles Pasqua" (May 30, 1987, p. 10).

72. *Le Monde* characterized the holding of the meeting as "a stone thrown into the garden" of Socialist President Mitterrand by the Chirac government, which the former was "forced" to approve publicly. Ibid.

73. Ibid.

74. *Washington Post*, May 29, 1987, p. A27.

75. *Le Monde*, May 30, 1987, p. 10.

76. Ibid.

77. *New York Times*, June 10, 1987, p. A10.

78. See, for example, *Washington Post*, June 10, 1987, p. A1.

79. *New York Times*, June 10, 1987, p. A1.

Chapter 3

1. *New York Times*, March 3, 1981, p. A5.

2. Ibid., March 7, 1981, p. A3.

3. Ibid., March 9, 1981, p. A1.

4. Ibid., March 13, 1981, p. A1.

5. Ibid., March 15, 1981, p. A1.

6. Ibid., March 8, 1981, p. A3.

7. British Broadcasting Corporation report, March 10, 1981, of Telegraph Agency of the Soviet Union broadcast (in Russian) for abroad, 1558 GMT, 8 March 1981.

8. British Broadcasting Corporation report, March 9, 1981, of Bakhtar news agency broadcast in England, 0455 GMT, 8 March 1981.

9. British Broadcasting Corporation report, March 10, 1981, of Karachi home service broadcast (in Urdu), 1500 GMT, 8 March 1981.

10. British Broadcasting Corporation report, March 10, 1981, of Kabul home service broadcast (in Pashto), 1530 GMT, 8 March 1981.

11. *New York Times*, March 16, 1981, p. A8.

12. *Washington Post*, March 17, 1981, p. A1.

13. Ibid.

14. *New York Times*, April 26, 1981, sec. 1, p. 11.

15. *The Times* (London), May 19, 1981, p. 9.

16. Foreign Broadcast Information Service report, June 16, 1981, of Karachi Domestic Service (in English), 1005 GMT, 13 June 1981.

17. Quoted in Chamberlain, "Collective Suspension of Air Services," 628.

18. Department of State cable no. USUN 3081, October 28, 1982 (unclassified).

19. Chamberlain, "Collective Suspension of Air Services," 628.

20. British Broadcasting Corporation report, December 4, 1982, of Bakhtar broadcast (in English), 0426 GMT, 3 December 1982.

21. *The Times* (London), July 14, 1984, p. 4.

22. Reuters report, November 7, 1986; interviews with U.S. Department of State officials.

23. *The Times* (London), November 27, 1981, p. 1.

24. Ibid., November 30, 1981, p. 6.

25. *Facts on File* 41, no. 2142 (December 1981), 909–10.

26. *The Times* (London), December 4, 1981.

27. Ibid.

28. U.S. Department of State, *American Foreign Policy: Current Documents, 1981, Supplement*, doc. #1798 (Department of State Daily Press Briefing, Thursday, December 3, 1981).

29. *The Times* (London), December 5, 1981, p. 4.

30. Interviews with U.S. and UK officials.

31. *The Times* (London), December 7, 1981, p. 4.

32. Ibid., January 6, 1982, p. 4.

33. *The Times* (London), July 28, 1982, p. 1.

34. A partial list compiled by the U.S. Federal Aviation Agency in February 1987 showed a total of 17 outstanding hijacking cases involving 9 countries in which the status of the hijackers was unknown or in which the hijackers had been granted asylum.

35. Department of State, *Patterns of Global Terrorism: 1985*, pp. 19, 36.

36. FBIS Middle East Report, June 17, 1985, p. A1, "Communiqué No. 2," Algiers Domestic Service (in Arabic), 1120 GMT, 15 June 1985.

37. FBIS Middle East Report, June 17, 1985, p. A2, "Birri Orders Hostages Transferred" (Clandestine), Radio Free Lebanon (in English), 1330 GMT, 17 June 1985.

38. *New York Times*, June 30, 1985, sec. 1, p. 1.

39. U.S. Department of State Press Release No. 145, July 1, 1985, Press Conference, the Honorable George P. Shultz, Secretary of State, at the White House, Sunday, June 30, 1985, 6:20 P.M., p. 5.

40. Ibid.

41. *New York Times*, July 22, 1985, pp. A1, A6.

42. FBIS Middle East Report, July 2, 1985, p. G1, "Officials to Protest Measures," Ihdin Radio of Free and Unified Lebanon (in Arabic), 1000 GMT, 2 July 1985; FBIS Middle East Report, July 3, 1985, p. G2, "Ambassador Protests U.S. Measures," Beirut Domestic Service (in Arabic), 1900 GMT, 2 July 1985.

43. Ibid.

44. U.S. Department of State, Press Release No. 145.

45. *New York Times*, July 2, 1985, p. A6.

46. Presidential Determination 85-14, *Federal Register*, July 1, 1985.

47. The laws in question are the Anti-Hijacking Act of 1974, Public Law No. 93-866, 88 Stat. 409, and sections 2001 and 2002 of the Comprehensive Crime Control Act of 1984, Public Law No.

98-473, 98 Stat. 2186. For an example of investigative activities of FBI agents during the hostage crisis, see FBIS Europe Report, July 1, 1985, p. S1, "FBI Agents Said to Investigate Hijacking," Athens *Elevtherotipia* (in Greek), 29 June 1985, p. 4.

48. See, for example, FBIS Middle East Report, July 3, 1985, p. G4, "Countermeasures Considered," Madrid EFE (in Spanish), 1815 GMT, 2 July 1985.

49. FBIS Middle East Report, July 9, 1985, p. G2, "Haydar Denies Amal Protecting Hijackers" (Clandestine), Radio Free Lebanon (in Arabic), 1945 GMT, 6 July 1985.

50. FBIS Middle East Report, July 12, 1985, "Names of TWA Hijackers Submitted to Authorities," Beirut Domestic Service (in Arabic), 0803 GMT, 12 July 1985.

51. FBIS Middle East Report, July 12, 1985, "Birri on Trying Hijackers," Beirut Voice of Lebanon (in Arabic), 1115 GMT, 12 July 1985.

52. See, for example, FBIS Western Europe Report, June 21, 1985, p. Q1, "Howe Expresses Support for U.S. in Hostage Crisis," London Press Association (in English), 0946 GMT, 21 June 1985; FBIS Western Europe Report, June 24, 1985, p. L3, "Government Informed on Lebanon Hostage Issue," Rome International Service (in Italian), 1730 GMT, 22 June 1985; FBIS Middle East Report, June 26 1985, p. G1, "Italian Envoy on EEC Concern," Paris AFP (in English), 1317 GMT, 25 June 1985; FBIS Western Europe Report, June 28, 1985, p. K1, "Dumas Discusses TWA Hostages, Gorbachev Visit," Paris Domestic Service (in French), 0540 GMT, 27 June 1985.

53. See, for example, FBIS Western Europe Report, July 1, 1985, p. A1, "ICAO Drafts Plan to Tighten Airport Security," Hong Kong AFP (in English), 0211 GMT, 28 June 1985; ibid., "France Urges Improving of Aviation Security," Paris Diplomatic Information Service (in French), 1245 GMT, 28 June 1985.

54. See, for example, FBIS Western Europe Report, July 2, 1985, p. J1, "Kohl Hails Reagan 'Success' on Hostage Release," Hamburg DPA (in German), 1323 GMT, 1 July 1985.

55. FBIS Western Europe Report, June 26, 1985, p. J3, "Focuses on Terrorism Issue," *Die Welt* (in German), June 26, 1985, p. 8.

56. *Washington Post*, July 22, 1985, p. A15.

57. Ibid.

58. Under the U.S.-West German extradition treaty (June 20,

1978, 32 U.S.T. 1485; T.I.A.S. 9785) either side had the right to refuse extradition for a crime for which the death penalty could be applied in the requesting state if the requested state did not permit the death penalty for a similar offense, unless the requesting state provided satisfactory assurances that the death penalty would not be carried out in a particular case. Air piracy carries a possible death penalty in the United States, but not in West Germany; eventually the United States did provide assurances that the death penalty would not be imposed if Hammadi was extradited.

59. See, for example, FBIS Western Europe Report, February 4, 1987, p. J1, "Quick Action on Hamadah Extradition Unlikely," *Frankfurter Rundschau* (in German), February 4, 1987, p. 1.

60. Transcript of President Reagan's News Conference in Venice, *Washington Post*, June 12, 1987.

61. Ibid., p. A20.

62. *Washington Post*, June 23, 1987, p. A12; June 25, 1987, p. A23.

63. *Department of State Bulletin* 87 (August 1987): 85.

64. *New York Times*, April 18, 1987, p. A1.

65. Ibid.

66. Ibid.

67. Ibid., A4.

68. Ibid., April 19, 1984, p. A1.

69. Ibid., April 23, 1987, p. A11.

70. Ibid., April 25, 1984, p. A10.

71. Ibid., April 27, 1984, p. A3.

72. *The Times* (London), April 30, 1987, p. 1.

73. See *New York Times*, April 24, 1984, p. A3, and April 25, 1984, p. A11.

74. *The Times* (London), April 25, 1984, p. 2.

75. Ibid., May 1, 1984, p. 1.

76. Ibid., May 2, 1984, p. 5.

77. Ibid., May 3, 1984, p. 6. A subsequent Italian proposal to establish a closer economic link between Libya and the EC was, however, vetoed by the British. Ibid., August 3, 1984, p. 6.

78. Ibid., May 15, 1984, p. 8.

79. Ibid., June 1, 1984, p. 4.

80. *New York Times*, April 26, 1984, p. A12. The Vienna Convention is discussed in more detail in Chapter 1.

81. *The Times* (London), April 30, 1984, p. 2, and May 3, 1984, p. 1.

82. *The Times* (London), June 21, 1984, p. 1.

83. *Diplomatic Privileges and Immunities: Government Report on Review of the Vienna Convention on Diplomatic Relations and Reply to "The Abuse of Diplomatic Immunities and Privileges"* (London: HMSO, 1985), 7.

84. Ibid.

85. Ibid.

86. Ibid., 8.

87. See U.S. Department of State, *American Foreign Policy, 1977–1980* (Washington, D.C.: GPO, 1981), 599–604 (Statement by the Under Secretary of State for Political Affairs (David Newsom) before the Special Subcommittee to Investigate Individuals Representing Interests of Foreign Governments of the Senate Judiciary Committee, August 4, 1980.

88. Jeffrey P. Bialos and Kenneth I. Juster, "The Libyan Sanctions: A Rational Response to State-Sponsored Terrorism?" *Virginia Journal of International Law* 26 (Summer 1986): 804.

89. See, for example, Secretary Shultz's address before the Jonathan Institute Conference on International Terrorism, June 24, 1984, reprinted in *Department of State Bulletin* 84 (August 1984): 31; Address of President Reagan before the Annual Convention of the American Bar Association, July 8, 1985, reprinted in U.S. Department of State, *American Foreign Policy: 1985*, p. 284; and the address of Ambassador Robert B. Oakley, director of the State Department Office for Counter-Terrorism, before the Issues Management Association, September 13, 1985, reprinted in *Department of State Bulletin* 85 (November 1985): 61.

90. U.S. Department of State, *Patterns of Global Terrorism: 1985*, p. 40.

91. See *New York Times*, November 25, 1985, p. A1.

92. *Department of State Bulletin* 86 (March 1986): 36 (President Reagan's opening statement, January 7, 1986).

93. Ibid., 37–38. Of course, a range of other political factors, particularly concern over Libyan meddling in Chad, had also helped stiffen U.S. official attitudes toward the Qadhafi government.

94. Ibid., 36–37.

95. Ibid., 38.

96. *The Times* (London), January 8, 1986, p. 5.

97. Ibid., January 23, 1986, p. 7.

98. Ibid., January 29, 1986, p. 6.

99. Tim Zimmerman, "The American Bombing of Libya," *Survival* (May/June 1987): 205.

100. *The Times* (London), April 7, 1986, p. 7.

101. Ibid., 1.

102. *The Times* (London), April 14, 1986, p. 1.

103. Ibid.

104. White House Statement, April 14, 1986, reprinted in *Department of State Bulletin* 86 (June 1986): 1.

105. President's Address to the Nation, April 14, 1986, reprinted in ibid.

106. Letter dated April 14, 1986 from the Acting Permanent Representative of the United States of America to the United Nations addressed to the President of the Security Council, U.N. Doc. S/17990, 14 April 1986. The relevant portion of Article 51 of the UN Charter is as follows: "Nothing in the present Charter shall impair the inherent right of individual or collective self-defense if an armed attack occurs against a member of the United Nations. . . ." Article 2(4) states: "All Members shall refrain in their international relations from the threat or use of force against the territorial integrity or political independence of any State, or in any other manner inconsistent with the purposes of the United Nations." Charter of the United Nations, 59 Stat. 101, TS 993.

107. *The Times* (London), April 14, 1986, p. 1.

108. *Time*, April 28, 1986, p. 24.

109. Ibid.

110. *The Times* (London), April 18, 1986, p. 1.

111. Ibid., April 28, 1986, p. 1.

112. Secretary Weinberger, at Joint News Conference by Secretary Shultz and Secretary Weinberger, April 14, 1986, reprinted in *Department of State Bulletin* 86 (June 1986): 6.

113. "Worldnet" Interview with Secretary Shultz, April 16, 1986, reprinted in ibid., 11.

114. "The Today Show" Interview with Secretary Shultz, April 15, 1986, reprinted in ibid., 7.

115. "Face the Nation" Interview with Secretary Shultz, reprinted in ibid., 18.

116. American Journalists' Interview with Secretary Shultz, April 17, 1986, reprinted in ibid., 14.

117. Joint News Conference by Secretary Shultz and Secretary Weinberger, April 14, 1986, reprinted in ibid., 5.

118. "Worldnet" Interview with Secretary Shultz, April 16, 1986, reprinted in ibid., 12.

119. *The Times* (London), April 18, 1986, p. 8.

120. Ibid., 10.

121. Ibid., 1.

122. Reprinted in *Department of State Bulletin* 86 (June 1986): 1.

123. *The Times* (London), April 18, 1986, p. 8.

124. Ibid., 7. In 1985 Libya had received thousands of tons of grain, milk, beef, and butter from the EC, all at subsidized prices.

125. Ibid., April 24, 1986, p. 7.

126. Ibid.

127. *Department of State Bulletin* 86 (June 1986): 23.

128. *The Times* (London), April 25, 1986, p. 1.

129. *The Economist*, April 26, 1986, p. 48.

130. *Time*, April 28, 1986, p. 18.

131. Edward Schumacher, "The United States and Libya," *Foreign Affairs* 65 (Winter 1986/87): 345.

132. Ibid., 28.

133. *Newsweek*, April 28, 1986, p. 22.

134. *The Times* (London), April 28, 1986, p. 5.

135. *Department of State Bulletin* 86 (June 1986): 19.

136. *The Times* (London), April 24, 1986, p. 4.

137. *Time*, April 28, 1986, p. 26.

138. *The Times* (London), April 29, 1986, p. 7.

139. At that time Libya was the sixteenth largest importer from the EC and the tenth largest exporter to it (the latter almost entirely oil); Libya was Italy's largest supplier of oil and West Germany's third largest. *The Economist*, April 26, 1986, p. 48.

140. *The Times* (London), April 24, 1986, p. 4.

141. "Face the Nation" Interview with Secretary Shultz, April 27, 1986, reprinted in *Department of State Bulletin* 86 (June 1986): 18.

142. Presentation by Ambassador Robert B. Oakley to the American Bar Association Panel on Background and Trends in Terrorism, Washington, D.C., June 6, 1986, p. 4.

143. Letters of Secretary of State George P. Shultz to Senator Richard G. Lugar, chairman of the Senate Committee on Foreign Relations, and to Congressman Dante B. Fascell, chairman of the House Committee on Foreign Affairs, June 30, 1986, reprinted in *The American Journal of International Law* 80 (1986): 950.

144. Schumacher, "The United States and Libya," 341; Bialos and Juster, "The Libyan Sanctions," 843–46.

145. *The Economist*, April 11, 1987, p. 34.

146. *The Times* (London), April 18, 1986, p. 1 and April 19, 1986, p. 1.

147. Ibid., May 9, 1986, p. 9 and May 12, 1986, p. 1.

148. U.S. Department of State, Bureau of Public Affairs Special Report No. 157, "Syrian Support for International Terrorism: 1983–1986," December 1986.

149. *Facts on File*, May 23, 1986, p. 371.

150. *The Times* (London), October 7, 1986, p. 1.

151. Ibid., October 25, 1986, p. 4.

152. Ibid., 5.

153. Ibid., 1.

154. Ibid.

155. Ibid., 5.

156. Ibid., October 26, 1986, p. 1.

157. Ibid., October 28, 1986, pp. 1, 9.

158. "Raimond on Plans to Accept Antiterrorism Proposals," FBIS Western Europe Report, November 10, 1986, p. K5, Paris AFP (in English), 1701 GMT, 7 November 1986.

159. *The Times* (London), November 11, 1986, pp. 1, 9.

160. *Department of State Bulletin* 87 (January 1987): 79.

161. *The Times* (London), November 12, 1986, p. 9.

162. "Discuss Arms, Terrorism," FBIS Western Europe Report, November 21, 1986, p. K1, Paris International Service (in French), 1300 GMT, 21 November 1986; *The Times* (London), November 26, 1986, p. 6.

163. *The Times* (London), October 25, 1986, p. 4.

164. See ibid., 5.

165. *The Times* (London), November 12, 1986, p. 1.

166. *The Economist*, July 18, 1987, p. 38.

167. *Washington Post*, September 3, 1987, p. A25.

Chapter 4

1. Putnam and Bayne, *Hanging Together: The Seven-Power Summits*, 21.

Index